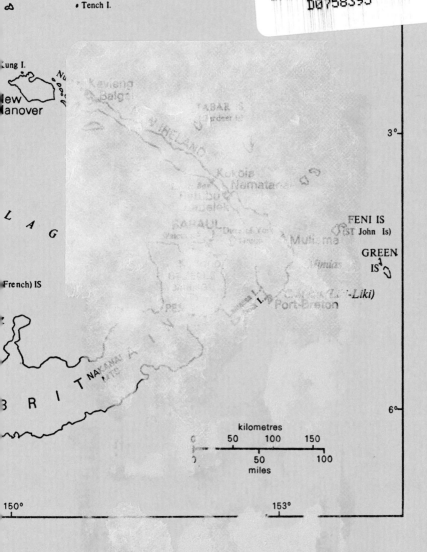

150°

Tench I.

Kung I.

New Hanover

Kavieng
Balgai

TABAR IS

NEW IRELAND

Kokola
Namatanai

FENI IS
(ST John Is)

RABAUL

Mulioma

GREEN IS

L A G

Nimias

(French) IS

Port-Breton

PE

NAKANAI MTS

B R I T

kilometres
0   50   100   150
0   50   100
miles

3°

6°

150°   153°

The New Guinea Memoirs of
Jean Baptiste Octave Mouton

Jean Baptiste Octave Mouton
Photograph supplied by Mrs J. Sturrock

General Editor: H. E. Maude

Pacific History Series No. 7

The New Guinea Memoirs of Jean Baptiste Octave Mouton

Edited, with an Introduction by
Peter Biskup

THE UNIVERSITY PRESS OF HAWAII HONOLULU

*The University Press of Hawaii,
Honolulu*

First published in Australia 1974

*Printed in Australia for the
Australian National University Press,
Canberra*

*Introduction and annotations © 1974
by Peter Biskup*

ISBN 0 8248 0328 0

Library of Congress Card no. 74 76379

Pacific History Series

The Pacific History Series of books provides an outlet for the publication of original manuscripts important to historians and others interested in the Pacific Islands.

1. *A Cruize in a Queensland Labour Vessel to the South Seas,* by W. E. Giles, edited by Deryck Scarr (1968)

2. *The Works of Ta'unga. Records of a Polynesian Traveller in the South Seas, 1833-1896,* by R. G. and Marjorie Crocombe (1968)

3. *The Trading Voyages of Andrew Cheyne, 1841-1844,* edited by Dorothy Shineberg (1971)

4. *A Residence of Eleven Years in New Holland and the Caroline Islands,* by James F. O'Connell, edited by Saul H. Riesenberg (1972)

5. *The South Sea Islanders and the Queensland Labour Trade,* by W. T. Wawn, edited by Peter Corris (1973)

6. *The Marquesan Journal of Edward Robarts, 1797-1824,* edited by Greg Dening (1974)

Foreword

Readers of the first six volumes of the Pacific History Series will have gained a variety of first-hand pictures of the island-studded crescent of Oceania stretching from the Polynesian Marquesas in the east, through Tahiti, the Cook Islands and Samoa, to Melanesian New Caledonia in the south-west and thence up through the New Hebrides and Solomons to the Micronesian Carolines.

The theme common to these often dramatic scenes has been the dynamic one of a world of small and isolated societies thrown into ferment by the impact of expatriate visitors or would-be residents on tradition-sanctioned mores. This seemingly inexorable process of culture change has been viewed through the eyes of beach-combers, a missionary, a trading captain and labour recruiters, who saw it with feelings varying from antipathy to whole-hearted approval.

In publishing the manuscript autobiography of Jean Baptiste Octave Mouton our locale moves west to New Ireland and New Britain, now politically part of Papua New Guinea, and our occupational categories of cultural agents are enlarged by the accession of one who was successively a settler, trader, planter and entrepreneur.

Mouton's manuscript is an opportune find since it fills in with his detailed personal experiences so much of the absorbing but often obscure history of the Marquis de Rays' ill-conceived colonisation venture in New Ireland and the early commercial development of the New Guinea island area now centred on Rabaul. The matter-of-fact, impassive style in which he depicts his relations with some of the most colourful characters in Pacific history, such as Farrell, Queen Emma and the Marquis himself, lends credence to the objectivity of his narrative. While he is clearly mistaken or forgetful at times, one feels that he is never deliberately misleading.

In his Introduction and Notes Peter Biskup not only enables the general reader to follow the thread of Mouton's memoirs with ease but makes a scholarly contribution himself to the early history of what came to be German New Guinea. With his European background, his polyglot linguistic attainments, and his knowledge of New Guinea gained as Senior Lecturer at the Administrative Staff College in Port Moresby from 1965 to 1969 and as co-author of *A Short History of New Guinea* and *Readings in New Guinea History*, he is well-qualified to identify the persons, places and episodes with which Mouton was connected. The References are of special value to students, since so many of the primary sources relating to the area and period were published in Germany or France and are only known to a handful of specialists.

As General Editor I have long regretted the paucity of unpublished sources relating to New Guinea suitable for this Series, and am

correspondingly elated at a fortuitous discovery
of the calibre of Mouton's memoirs. It is to be
hoped that with the establishment of the
Papua New Guinea Documents Project, under
the aegis of the Pacific Manuscripts Bureau,
more narratives of interest and importance
will come to light. Any that do will be examined
carefully with an eye to inclusion.

H. E. Maude

Contents

Maps

Introduction

Jean Baptiste Octave Mouton was born in 1866 in the French-speaking part of Belgium. He came from an impecunious *petit bourgeois* family and had left school at the age of eleven—a common enough experience for children of his background before the introduction in 1914 of compulsory education. At fourteen he migrated with his father for the Free Colony of Port-Breton, otherwise known as New France, with the last of the four expeditions to reach the shores of New Ireland.

The Moutons arrived in Port-Breton in August 1881 and remained there until the final evacuation of the settlement in February 1882. Together with perhaps a dozen of other undeterred individuals, they chose to remain in New Guinea rather than to return home, never to regret their decision. They settled as copra traders on the Gazelle Peninsula, initially under contract to Thomas Farrell and his part-Samoan common law wife, the quasi-legendary Queen Emma. In 1883 they changed over to Hernsheim and Co. and, after his father's death in 1888, Octave signed a contract

[1] Blum 1900: 151. All subsequent footnotes use this form of citation. Full bibliographical details of works cited can be found in the References.

with the Mioko agency of the Deutsche Handels- und Plantagengesellschaft, better known in the Pacific as the long-handle firm. In 1891 he planted the first ten hectares with coconut trees, on land acquired by his father some eight years earlier. By the mid-1890s Mouton became the first independent trader in German New Guinea; by getting his trade goods directly from Sydney (initially through the Sacred Heart Mission) and selling his copra to Burns, Philp and Co., he gradually managed to break the virtual foreign trade monopoly of the 'Big Three' mentioned above. He planted more coconut trees on his Kinigunan plantation, expanded his trading activities to northern New Ireland, Kapingamarangi and Ontong Java and by 1899 had become the envy of all the struggling traders and small planters. 'The example of this man,' said Blum, 'is noteworthy from the point of view of the development of the entire colony. He started with nothing and is now, as a result of his industry and clear-headedness, a prosperous man.'[1] In 1902 Mouton felt confident enough to leave his business interests in the hands of a manager and to visit Sydney on what proved to be only the first of several business-cum-pleasure trips to Australia. It was on one such occasion that he met a Sydney girl and married her in 1903; they had one son, Octave Max, born in 1904. It seems that he intended to live in Sydney—he bought a property at the National Park, not far from Port Hacking—but was forced to spend most of his time in New Guinea, since he could not rely on his managers. He divorced his wife in 1911 and remarried two years later; by his second wife, he had one son, Jean Leopold, born in 1915. After the war he divided his time about equally between Sydney and Kinigunan. In April 1929 he sold his plantation to the Sacred Heart

2

Mission for £80,000, and retired to the suburb of Bellevue Hill. But he did not sever all connections with the territory: in 1930 he bought the *Rabaul Times* and later formed Rabaul Recreations Ltd which ran Rabaul's only cinema. He died of cancer in Sydney in 1946 at the age of eighty.

Mouton's motives in writing the *Memoirs* can only be guessed at. They were almost certainly not meant for publication, at any rate not in the form in which they appear in this book. Mouton wrote in retirement—to pass the time, perhaps, or to cure that bittersweet nostalgia which seems to grip most of those who, having spent the best years of their lives in the tropics, retire to rusticate in more temperate climes. It is equally difficult to decide when he wrote them—there are no clues in the *Memoirs* themselves except for the fact that they end early in 1931. It may be that Mouton was inspired by the publication, in 1936, of Madame Niau's *The Phantom Paradise*, the first comprehensive (if not always accurate) account in English of the Port-Breton disaster. This supposition is lent some weight by the fact that there exists an incomplete French version of the reminiscences written soon after 1911 and covering much the same ground as the later English version. The appearance of *The Phantom Paradise* may have reminded Mouton of his earlier literary efforts; perhaps he dug up the manuscript, rewrote it in English and expanded it to cover his last twenty years in New Guinea. What tells against this line of reasoning are the occasional discrepancies in dates, distances and other minor details between the two versions, not to mention the fact that several incidents described in the French version have been omitted from the English version and vice versa. It is also not unreasonable to assume

3

that, had the *Memoirs* been written after 1936 rather than in the early 1930s (as seems likely), Mouton would have mentioned, at least in passing, such events as his third marriage or the marriage of his first son, Octave Max, both of which had occurred before 1936.

Whatever their origin, the *Memoirs* are a valuable addition to early New Guineana: unlike the pioneer missionaries and government officials, the early traders tended to be an inarticulate lot and left few records for posterity. Admittedly, Mouton sat down to write many years after most of the events he describes had taken place, so that the usual allowances must be made for lapses of memory, resulting not only in mistakes of fact but also in selective coverage of events in general. But the *Memoirs* are not an autobiography in the usual sense. Mouton does not, as a rule, attempt to justify his actions or even to explain them; he writes without undue emotion or involvement. Describing the expedition to punish the villagers who took part in the 1893 attack on Ralum Plantation and the New Guinea Company station at Kokopo (the Germans called it Herbertshoehe), he says: 'It was at that patch that I managed to drop a fellow with white feathers on his head and a round disc on his chest he was about three hundred yards, all I can say is that we saw him drop and then next the blood, the wounded was carried away.' It is this combination of detachment and attention to detail which at times gives Mouton's reminiscences a directness and freshness usually found only in actual *reportage*; his descriptions of daily life at Port-Breton, of the physical dangers the pioneer traders had to face, of his early recruiting trips, give one the feeling that the events he talks about took place but

4

yesterday. Only occasionally does emoti[on]
show—as when he remembers how he w[as]
once offered a piece of baked human fle[sh]
served with taro and bananas, which loo[ked]
like pork and which turned him off pork [for]
years to come. Nor does he always disgu[ise]
hatred for some of his contemporaries,
particularly his *bête noire*, Thomas Farrell[,]
but then he was not alone in his unflatter[ing]
estimate of the latter's character and busi[ness]
practices.

Mouton himself emerges from his remin[is-]
cences as a down-to-earth, pragmatic and
somewhat colourless person, a calculating
money-maker who lived largely for his bus[iness]
and his plantation. His New Guinea conte[m-]
poraries must have seen him in much the s[ame]
light for, unlike some of the more flamboy[ant]
New Britain pioneers, he hardly rates a
mention in the literature of the period. His
Australian acquaintances and friends, on t[he]
other hand, remember him as a 'kind and
lovable fellow', generous with his money. C[an]
these two views be reconciled? I think they
can. Mouton never really mastered the Engl[ish]
language. He is at his best when he talks ab[out]
concrete, everyday things and events; his
occasional excursions into the realm of the
abstract tend to end in confusion.
His reticence to discuss his personal life is
understandable. He may have blamed himse[lf]
for the failure of his first marriage (it seems
that his wife consoled herself during his long
absences in New Guinea with the caretaker o[f]
their National Park property) and he was
somewhat disappointed in his sons. Yet from
the French version (written while he was still
with his first wife) one gets a different impression of Mouton the individual. He seems to
write without an emotional strait-jacket and,
while the occasional grammatical or spelling

5

mistakes are still there, he is more at ease when discussing ideas and relationships. As for the views of his New Guinea contemporaries, these can to some extent be explained by the fact that Mouton was not a member of the social establishment: his strained relations with Queen Emma ensured that he was not on the guest list of her Gunantambu 'castle' and because of his poor German and his educational background he had little in common with the local New Guinea Company or the Imperial officials.

Although the *Memoirs* are not well structured, they can nevertheless be divided into several parts. The first, which covers slightly less than one-third of the text, describes Mouton's childhood, the sea voyage to Port-Breton and the six months he spent there. The second part is considerably shorter and could well be entitled 'Pioneering on the Gazelle Peninsula': we learn about the copra trade, the early land purchases and the clashes with the local people. The next section (about one-third of the text) is mainly about Mouton's life as plantation owner, his recruiting trips to New Ireland and his rise as the first independent trader; it also contains comments on Tolai customs. The remainder is a highly selective account of the years starting with Mouton's first marriage in 1902 and ending with the sale of his plantation in 1929. The background information which follows may help the reader place Mouton's observations in a wider context.

The Free Colony of Port-Breton, better known as New France, was not the first attempt before the 1884 partition to plant a European settlement in New Guinea. As early as 1793 Captain John Hayes of the East India Company, with the private backing of three

Calcutta merchants, established a semi-official colony called New Albion near today's Manokwari in West Irian. The settlement was evacuated after twenty-one months, and cost the lives of more than a dozen Europeans and Indian soldiers. In 1828 the Dutch, following the annexation of the south-west coast of New Guinea, opened a Government post at Triton Bay, naming it Merkusoord, in honour of the then Governor of the Moluccas. The settlement was closed in 1835 after it had claimed the lives of over one hundred Dutch officials and Indonesian soldiers and their dependents. Other colonising projects failed to get off the ground: some prospective settlers could not raise the required capital while others, for instance Brigadier-General Henry McIver and his 'adventurers' of the New Guinea Exploration and Colonisation Company, abandoned their plans because of Colonial Office opposition.

New France differed from these schemes in its scale, its entirely private nature and the personality and motives of its founder. The organisers of New France managed to raise nine million francs (about £370,000); by comparison, British New Guinea was to be run for many years on an annual budget of no more than £25,000 and the German New Guinea Company was to spend even less on its administrative—as distinct from purely economic—activities. All told, between 1879 and 1881 some 700 settlers left for New Guinea, in four separate expeditions; about half of them died in New Guinea or at sea, some seventy returned to Europe, about 200 settled in New South Wales and Queensland and only about a dozen remained in New Guinea. Because of the unco-operative attitude of the French Government, all four expeditions had to leave from non-French ports. The first ship,

[2] Niau 1936: p. 26.
[3] Ibid.: p. 11.

the *Chandernagor*, was prevented from leaving Le Havre by a decree of the Ministry of Trade and Agriculture and had to be diverted first to Antwerp and then to Flushing; the *Génil*, the *India* and the *Nouvelle Bretagne* left from Barcelona. As for the founder of New France, Charles Bonaventure du Breuil, better known as the Marquis de Rays, authorities disagree whether he was a swindler, a madman or both. A swindler the Marquis certainly was; he sold land he did not own: 'lands unknown were represented as known; waste tracts or marshy plains . . . were made to seem as if they were groaning under the weight of bountiful crops of coconuts, with copra only waiting to be gathered and transported . . .'.[2] His madness— if indeed he was mad—lay in his insistence that the scheme must go on (and human life be sacrificed) when it was all too evident that it could not succeed. But he was also a dreamer, a deeply religious man, a Don Quixote bent on recapturing the 'glory that was France'.[3] He reminds one of another dreamer, Napoleon III, who had nearly ruined France a few years earlier; there was even a certain physical resemblance between the two. The Marquis' arrest in Spain in July 1882 was seen by many of his adherents as an act of political and religious persecution, and even in Port-Breton some settlers did not think him guilty, in spite of all the evidence before their eyes. French courts took a different view. After his extradition from Spain the Marquis was tried and sentenced in January 1884 to four years' imprisonment and a fine of 3000 francs. He died before his sentence expired.

Although the Marquis had never visited New Ireland, he was a much-travelled man and had lived for varying periods outside Europe. He was born in Brittany in 1832, and came from a noble family of ancient Celtic

8

stock. Colonising and adventure seem to have been in his blood (some of his ancestors had served with distinction in French colonial administration), for he was nicknamed *le petit colon* by his schoolmates. Not yet twenty, he had tried his luck as a rancher in the United States of America. Subsequently he was a peanut broker in Senegal and also lived for a period in Madagascar and Indochina. In 1869 he returned to the family property in Barnabec, by then heavily mortgaged, became a model husband and joined the Legitimist Party which was opposed to all the Third Republic stood for. But the quiet and respectable life of a country squire did not apparently agree with him. In July 1877 there appeared in several French newspapers a brief advertisement in the name of Monsieur du Breuil de Rays, offering land in the Free Colony of Port-Breton at five francs a hectare and promising investors a 'quick fortune without leaving one's homeland'. It is not generally known that the original Port-Breton was to be planted at Shark Bay, one of the least hospitable stretches of Western Australian coastline, selected, it would seem, because the names of French discoveries abounded in the region. We intend to found, announced the Marquis in his prospectus,

a free institution designed for the vast expansion of Colonial enterprise. The vast solitudes of Australia throughout the North-West, adjoining our settlement (Port Breton), belong to no one. No Government has any claim on these vast tracts, partly discovered by the French nation; no savage people and no settled tribe cultivates the ground—only a few wandering families of timid blacks pass over the limitless waste. The land belongs to the first occupier. It is

9

[4] Collingridge 1923: 14.
[5] Ibid.
[6] Duperrey, I. I.
Voyage autour du Monde,
Paris, 1825-30, quoted
in Michener and Day
1957: 64.

only necessary to settle in sufficient number
to organise upon a sound basis, and with
sufficient means, under a Government
agreed upon and accepted beforehand. We
now ask you for means, and we now offer
you this Government. To us, then, belongs
the future. On the ocean shore of a new
port and a new country we shall establish
the perpetuity of our families and hand
down our memory to posterity.[4]

It is indicative of the Marquis' mentality
and lack of realism that he was 'quite
astounded'[5] when one of the recipients of this
document, an Australian living at Fontenay
aux Roses, near Paris, told him that neither
the British nor the Western Australian
Government would countenance such a
scheme. Sometime in 1878, after an official
communication from the British Ambassador
at Paris had finally convinced him that he
would not be allowed to plant his Utopia in
Western Australia, the Marquis moved Port-
Breton to Port-Praslin, named by Bougainville
in 1768 and visited by Duperrey and his staff
of scientists in August 1823. During the nine
days he spent in southern New Ireland,
Duperrey found the local people friendly
enough, and experienced unusually clement
weather for that time of the year. If the Marquis
had chosen Port-Praslin on the basis of the
published accounts of the expedition—as
seems to be the case—he could not have read
them very carefully, for they warned of the
possibility of torrential rain and spoke of a
'mass of vegetation' which left 'no clear spot'
and covered 'the whole place with a single,
vast forrest'.[6] Bougainville, who had visited
Port-Praslin in July, referred to 'continual
rain' and described the country as 'mountain-
ous, the soil is very light, and the rocks are

[7] Bougainville 1772: 332-34.
[8] Baudouin 1885: 143.
[9] Ibid: 146.

hardly covered with it'.[7] Worse than that, Port-Praslin turned out to be an unhealthy *cul-de-sac*, with an annual rainfall close to 200 inches (the settlers called it *le trou*, meaning the hole, as well as some other more expressive and down-to-earth names). During the rainy season (April to September), downpours would last up to a week; when it did not rain, the air 'seemed to stagnate like the vapours in a sweating room',[8] because the island of Lambom prevented the south-easterly winds from reaching 'the hole'. During the Dry, life was more bearable but the prevailing north-westerlies gave little relief, since they were deflected by the mountain range behind the port. The peculiar topography of the locality, combined with the poor quality of the soil, made agriculture virtually impossible. Even the *taro*, the staple food of southern New Ireland, refused to thrive; it 'shot up high in search of light, but would not set'.[9]

In selecting Port-Praslin as the seat of his empire (it was to include not only New Ireland but also the rest of today's Territory of Papua and New Guinea and the British Solomons), the Marquis had in fact chosen one of the few spots anywhere in New Guinea to be avoided at all costs. 'The tragedy of Nouvelle France,' said Michener in his well-written though not always accurate account of the reign of Charles I, Emperor of Oceania (a title the Marquis assumed in 1880), 'can best be comprehended with the aid of the map. Mark in red pencil each of the New Ireland establishments where Germans and Englishmen have lived prosperously . . . The red dots are scattered fairly evenly along the entire coast. This means that a gambler could have pointed to almost any spot along the shore, saying, "That's where we'll settle." And his chances of striking a likely site—move up or down the coast ten

11

[10] Michener and Day 1957: 74-75.
[11] Baudouin 1885: 15.
[12] Translation of speech in Niau, 1936: 11-14; original in *La Colonie Libre de Port-Breton, 1879* and in de Groote 1880.

miles in either direction—would have been almost one hundred per cent certain.'[10]

But to return to the story. By the beginning of 1879, with Port-Breton definitely situated in New Ireland, some 3000 people had bought about 500,000 francs worth of land in the non-existent colony. But this was not enough for the enterprising Marquis, who now thought in terms of millions rather than thousands. The instalment of the first Republican (and anti-clerical) Ministry in February 1879 gave his scheme an unexpected boost. He decided to enlist the support of the Roman Catholic Church; in the words of the doctor of the last expedition, Dr Baudouin, the 'colony was to be catholic, which would not prevent it from being free, and it would be free, which would not prevent it from being catholic'.[11] The Government, as expected, refused to support or even condone the colony, thus blessing it in the eyes of the faithful. At a conference held in Marseilles in April 1879, the Marquis gave further details of his enlarged scheme. Land would be properly surveyed and entered into a cadastre, and the bonds representing ownership (*bons coloniaux* or *bons de terrain*) would be transferable like any other property. Agriculture was to be along the lines of the 'Dutch system' used in Java, with indentured Chinese, Indian and Malay coolies rather than 'enslaved negroes' providing the labour. New Guineans were to be given the benefits of Christianity and civilisation: 'the monks expelled from old France will help to Christianise the New.'[12]

Although the Marquis could promise no other security except 'the success of the enterprise', funds started to pour in—and the price of land went up first to ten francs a hectare, then to twenty francs and finally in April 1881 to fifty francs. Two months after the Marseilles conference there appeared the first issue of a fortnightly sheet, *La Nouvelle France*, devoted to the affairs of the colony-in-making and profusely illustrated by old engravings purporting to picture South Seas islands scenery. Prospective investors were showered with pamphlets and prospectuses. For a consideration, they could also procure a portrait of the Marquis (for sixty centimes), a map of Port-Breton (one franc), a map of New France, either in an 'ordinary' edition (fifty centimes) or in a 'de luxe' edition (one franc) and, finally, (for two francs) the 'March of Port-Breton', composed by the Liberian consul in Paris, one Dr Febrer, and dedicated to the founder of the colony.

But there was still one minor problem to be overcome: the Marquis had promised the subscribers that they could become rich without emigrating. He solved this difficulty by floating a second company, the Societé des Fermiers-Généraux de la Nouvelle-France. Anyone who owned shares in the parent company could join, by paying an additional five francs a share (representing one hectare of land). For this payment, the new company undertook to make the land productive with the help of indentured labour. Never one to do things half-way, the Marquis was also instrumental in the foundation of the Société des Sucreries, Distilleurs et Exploitation Agricole which was to run the Port-Breton sugar factory, the Societé Franco-Océanienne de Commerce et de Navigation which was to establish a regular shipping service between Australia and China, and the Societé Franco-Océanienne des Mines de Nouvelle-France which was to exploit the New Ireland copper deposits.

Matched against this grandiose vision, the real New France was a mundane, almost

13

grotesque affair—except for those who lost their lives or money there. Perhaps real is not the right word to use, for during much of the time between the arrival of the first settlers in January 1880 and the final evacuation of February 1882, the colony did not exist except on the pages of *La Nouvelle France*. The first ship, the sailing vessel *Chandernagor*, with some seventy settlers on board, reached Port-Praslin on 20 January 1880, having earlier disembarked seventeen colonists on the Laughlan Islands. On 31 January the settlement was 'moved' twelve miles east of Port-Praslin to Liki-Liki (also known as Metlik), in circumstances which help to explain much of the subsequent failure of the entire scheme. On 26 January there arose a violent storm, the Captain of the *Chandernagor* made for the open sea and, unable to land during the next five days, finally sought shelter at Liki-Liki. A group of settlers, including Titeu de la Croix, the first of the line of Governors who were to preside over the affairs of the unhappy colony, was left in Port-Praslin without supplies. Immediately after landing at Liki-Liki, the Captain of the *Chandernagor* sent a rescue party to fetch the stranded group, but they found the camp deserted. The colonists were eventually reunited on 7 February (a small group had reached Liki-Liki by canoe, while the remainder had made their way overland) and on the following day a general meeting ratified the choice of Liki-Liki as the 'main' settlement. A large square, named Place de la République, was pegged out, as well as a number of streets, and the settlers selected their land. Then the unloading of supplies began. There was ample evidence, said the Methodist Missionary, the Rev. George Brown, who visited Liki-Liki on several occasions,

[13] Brown 1908: 363.

of the great preparations which had been made in France for the success of the expedition. A large steam boiler and fireplace were on the beach, together with a great quantity of bricks, which were intended, I believe, to be used in the foundations of the cathedral which they purposed building. They also had the machinery for sugar refining, a steam crane, incubators, a sawmill, and agricultural implements; but it was evident that there had been great carelessness either in shipping the material or in landing it, as they had cases of knife handles without any blades, and a number of wheelbarrows, but no wheels. They had scarcely any axes, and the few spades with which they were supplied appeared to be of the worst possible material.[13]

Not only did the colonists lack basic equipment; they were also short of food. On 20 February the *Chandernagor*, with Titeu de la Croix on board, left Liki-Liki under the cover of darkness and sailed to Sydney for supplies. The Governor decided to 'abdicate' and remained in Sydney, never to set foot on New Ireland shores again. By the time the desperately-needed supplies arrived in mid-May (on a chartered schooner, the *Émilie*), forty-two of the sixty-six colonists left behind at Liki-Liki had been evacuated, at their request, to Port Hunter on the Duke of York Islands by the Methodist missionaries George Brown and Benjamin Danks. After the arrival of the *Émilie* a few of the evacuees rejoined their comrades at Liki-Liki, but by mid-August the entire contingent was back on the Duke of York Islands and Liki-Liki was 'officially' abandoned.

The next ship to leave Europe, the *Génil*, reached New Ireland late in August 1880. It

[14] Michener andDay 1957: 67.
[15] Brown 1908: 367.

had no settlers on board—they had all deserted in Singapore, in protest against the unorthodox disciplinary methods (said to have included the use of 'medieval torture instruments' and the stringing up of offenders by their thumbs)[14] employed by the Captain, Gustave Rabardy. The *Génil* reached Port-Praslin with a skeleton crew and twenty-five Malay coolies, engaged by Rabardy in Singapore, but did not unload its human cargo until the arrival of the third ship, the *India*, on 14 October. The *India* contingent consisted of 340 colonists, mostly Italians, of whom more than one-half were women and children. It was a much better organised expedition than the first two, and for a month or so it looked as if New France might succeed after all. The Captain of H.M.S. *Beagle*, which called at Port-Breton on 2 November, found everyone in good health and full of determination and ten days later the Rev. George Brown could still report 'good progress'.[15] But by the end of November demoralisation had set in, malaria and vitamin deficiencies began to take their toll, and provisions were running low. So the new Governor, Colonel J. A. le Prévost, proposed that he and Rabardy should go to Sydney for supplies, solemnly promising to be back in fifty days. Once in Sydney, the Colonel chose to follow the example of his predecessor, developed 'heart trouble' and New France was for the second time without a Governor. Rabardy did not return until 20 February, almost five weeks later than promised. He found Port-Breton deserted and the *India* gone—the decision to evacuate the settlement was apparently made only a day or two before the *Génil*'s return, and the two ships missed each other by only a few hours. On its way to Sydney the *India* called at Noumea where the French authorities found her unseaworthy;

[16] *Sydney Morning Herald*, 6 May 1881, quoted in Niau 1936: 69-70.
[17] Baudouin 1885: 92.

she was eventually sold for a fraction of what the Marquis had paid for her. The settlers were offered a home in New Caledonia but most of them had no wish to live in a penal colony. Some 200 were eventually brought to Sydney on the *James Patterson*, chartered for that purpose by the New South Wales Government, and decided to settle in Australia. But their trials were far from over. Fearing the creation of a 'colony within a colony', the New South Wales Government insisted that the group be split up (and friends and relatives separated from each other) so that they 'would more readily acquire a knowledge of the English language and English customs'.[16]

The Moutons left Barcelona on the *Nouvelle Bretagne* on 7 April 1881, the very day the dispirited *India* contingent disembarked in Sydney. By then the Liki-Liki fiasco, while not well publicised, was certainly no longer a secret, some of the survivors of the *Chandernagor* expedition having returned home before the end of 1880. But the fate of the *India* expedition was apparently still unknown; if the Marquis and his associates had any knowledge of the evacuation of Port-Breton, they kept it to themselves. The settlers on the *Nouvelle Bretagne* first heard the bad news at Colombo, where a cable from the Marquis awaited the Captain, Jules Henry, naming him 'provisional' Governor of New France. Captain Henry was one of the few realists among the colony's officials. In Singapore he and the French consul had tried in vain to dissuade the settlers from proceeding to Port-Breton. New France had become an obsession with most of them: 'they believed Captain Henry wanted to call off the expedition so that he alone could exploit the riches of New France and to steal— this was the word used by one man—their share of paradise.'[17] Having failed to divert

17

18 Ibid.: 101.
19 Niau 1936: 88.

his charges from their fixations, Captain
Henry proceeded to ensure that the expedition
be at least properly equipped: he bought tools
and food, engaged local carpenters, fishermen
and a group of 'Arab policemen', purchased
an old barque which was to be used as a
floating hospital and generally tried to replace
'decor by reality'.[18] In this he was fully supported by the ship surgeon, the young Dr
Baudouin: both men cared more about the
welfare of the people on board than the 'glory
that was France', and had displayed 'self-
sacrifice, skill and loyalty'[19] throughout the
expedition.

After his return to France, Dr Baudouin was
chief prosecution witness at the trial of the
Marquis and his associates and subsequently
published the book *L'Aventure de Port-Breton*,
generally accepted as the most reliable eye-
witness account of the Port-Breton affair.
Much of what has subsequently been written
about New France comes from this book, and
I myself have found it indispensable in editing
the first part of Mouton's reminiscences where
essential background information is often
lacking and where the sequence of events is
at times difficult to follow. This is not to say
that Mouton's account is inferior to that of Dr
Baudouin: it is different. Baudouin's comments
are those of an intellectual. He has a point
of view; he is critical; even when he chronicles
(as when he describes the deadly infighting
and intrigues among the leaders) he still looks
for motives and explanations. Mouton
describes the everyday life of an indentured
labourer's son; he writes about simple things
like leaking roofs, bug-infested beds and food—
especially food. It is only when it comes to
portraying people that Baudouin's account
can be said to be superior.

In Mouton's reminiscences, with one or two

[20] Baudouin 1885: 98.
[21] Ibid.: 162.

exceptions, the individual members of the *Nouvelle Bretagne* expedition are shadowy figures—and understandably so, since Mouton was only a boy when he knew them. Baudouin's book brings them to life, warts and all. Notary Chambaud, for instance, whose job it was to survey land and to preside over the civilian court, emerges from the book as a sinister individual who did precious little surveying or presiding over court proceedings but who took very seriously the task of 'inventorying and sealing up the chattels of the dead'.[20] Captain Rabardy, whose 'terrible character' is only vaguely hinted at by Mouton, becomes a frighteningly real paranoiac who insisted on dining alone in his cabin, with a loaded revolver always on the table, and who surrounded himself by a 'black guard' of Buka recruits.[21] We meet the Director-General of Agriculture, Schurman, who finds himself defeated by the hostile environment and spends most of his time tending exotic spices. We meet Abbé Deny, who went to Port-Breton determined to plant the cross on the smallest islands of the Pacific. We learn about the praetors of the military contingent, dreaming about creating a new state in the jungles of New Guinea, of establishing a string of forts along the coast, of daring expeditions into the interior. And we make the acquaintance of some of the lesser colonists, with their ingenious plans for getting rich quickly, including the one man who succeeded, up to a point, in putting his plan into practice. His name was de Splenter and he went to Port-Breton to establish a seaside hotel which would offer travellers the best in comfort and service. He managed to open a tiny canteen where he sold beer and wine bought from passing ships; unfortunately he was paid for his refreshments

19

[22] Being of recent origin, the term does not appear in the *Memoirs*; nor does Mouton use other names under which the Tolai were known, such as Gunantuna or Kuanua.

in the Port-Breton paper currency (*bons monétaires*) and so lost his entire investment.

When the Moutons landed in Mioko in February 1882, the golden days of the copra trade—when a ton of copra could be bought from the villagers for something like six shillings and sold in London for £20—were gone forever. Still, the opportunities for making a quick profit were there for anyone prepared to work hard and to put up with the climate and the lack of amenities. The coastal areas of the Gazelle Peninsula had been pacified and interhamlet warfare virtually eliminated, practically all the land was still in native hands and the number of Europeans settled there negligible. Conditions were ideal in other ways: because of its volcanic character much of the soil on the peninsula was extremely fertile, the local Tolai[22] population was one of the densest in Melanesia and had from pre-contact times a flair for trade, having been accustomed to producing more than they required for bare subsistence. Markets were conducted regularly, usually every three days, and the transactions were conducted through the medium of a shell currency known as *tambu* or *diwarra*.

At the time of the Moutons' arrival the European community in the Bismarck Archipelago (if the term community can be applied to the motley of individuals assembled there) comprised no more than twenty-five souls, mostly traders. There were two Methodist missionaries in the islands, the Rev. Benjamin Danks who arrived late in 1878, over three years after the landing of the founder of the mission, the Rev. George Brown, and the Rev. I. Rooney, who came in 1881. By 1882 the Methodists had got over most of the difficulties which normally accompany the establishment of a mission: they had bought about seventy acres of land in the Duke of York Islands, and had over twenty stations in the Duke of York group, on the Gazelle Peninsula and in southern New Ireland.

The traders were represented by three establishments: the Mioko branch of the Deutsche Handels- und Plantagengesell-schaft (Mouton refers to it as the Mioko Agency), Hernsheim and Co., and Thomas Farrell. The D.H.P.G. was the successor of the Hamburg merchant firm of Johann César Godeffroy and Son, established in 1766, which started trading in the Pacific in 1845, established its Pacific headquarters in Samoa in 1857 and had been active in New Guinea waters since 1871. In 1873 it landed a white trader on the Gazelle Peninsula and another on the island of Matupit, but they were driven out almost immediately. In 1875 it established a station at Mioko, this time permanently. In 1878 the Godeffroys transferred their South Seas interests to the newly formed D.H.P.G., but the parent company went bankrupt soon afterwards.

The D.H.P.G., at least in its New Guinea operations, lacked the vigour of its predecessor, and was soon displaced from its leading position by Hernsheim and Co. which made its appearance in the archipelago in 1875. The founder of this Company, Eduard Hernsheim, was the closest equivalent to a *pukka sahib* ever produced by the German colonies and his residence on Matupit was for many years the cultural headquarters of German New Guinea. A Hamburg seaman who started plying the West Pacific in the early 1870s, using Hongkong as his base, he established himself on Palau and Yap in the first half of 1874. Later in the year he went to the Hermit Islands to collect trepang, bought

21

[23] Kraemer 1927: 151.
[24] Wichmann 1910: 275.
[25] Truppel 1888: 287.

land at Port Hunter on the return journey, and in 1876 opened a station at Makada in the Duke of York Islands (it was moved to Matupit two years later). In the meantime he had been joined by his brother Franz; after about a year the latter returned to Hamburg and 'so came into existence the firm of Hernsheim and Co.', operating from Matupit.[23] In 1882 the company had over forty stations in New Britain, Northern New Ireland, the Admiralty and the Hermit Islands, and in the Carolines and the Marshall Islands; in 1887 it was to divest itself of its interests in the last-mentioned group in favour of the Jaluit Company.

The last of the 'Big Three' establishments in existence in 1882 was that of Thomas Farrell and his common-law wife Emma Elisabeth Forsayth. Farrell was, by universal acclaim, something of a 'dubious character',[24] one of the last of the South Seas pioneers 'whose stormy past and moral qualities do not bear a closer investigation'.[25] Of Irish stock, he had spent most of his younger days in Australia (he was still legally married to an Australian when he settled in New Guinea), had tried his luck on the New Zealand goldfields and was a shipowner and hotelkeeper in Apia when he met Emma in the mid-1870s. Emma, whose maiden name was Coe, was a Samoan half-blood, educated in San Francisco and Sydney by her American father, and had married the Mauritius-born Scotsman James Forsayth in 1869 at the age of nineteen. Vivacious and beautiful, she found herself at a loose end after the disappearance of her husband in a shipping disaster off the China coast in 1873, and when Farrell asked her to come with him to New Guinea, she agreed. The couple settled in Mioko late in 1878 as traders for the D.H.P.G., but almost from the start did much trading

22

[26] Australian Naval
Station 1881: 3.

on their own account. By mid-1881 Farrell
was independent, conducting his business in
partnership with the Sydney firm of Mason
Brothers. He was a thrusting entrepreneur and
ruthless with his competitors as well as his
own traders. According to Romilly, the
British Deputy Commissioner for the Western
Pacific, he failed to supply his traders with
European food, medicines or habitable houses,
paid them the merest pittance for wages and
only sent boats to visit them at rare intervals:

> The men he sends off to his outlying stations
> are, I imagine, the sweepings of the colonies,
> as I am convinced no respectable man,
> however reduced in circumstances, could
> accept such a life. About the antecedents of
> these men I was unable to obtain any
> information, but they invariably refuse
> every opportunity of leaving, in spite of the
> extreme unhealthiness of the climate, which
> usually kills them in less than two years.
> The two big German stations present a
> marked difference to the English. I was
> much struck with all Mr. Hernsheim's
> traders. They are all well-educated, gentle-
> menlike men, clean and neat in their dress.
> They live extremely well, and have all got
> good houses and serviceable boats . . . I am
> convinced that these natives, savages
> though they be, make a very great distinc-
> tion between the Germans and the English.[26]

It was the Moutons' misfortune that they
should have started life in New Britain as
traders for Farrell; however, as Octave points
out in his reminiscences, they had little choice
in the matter. When their contract with
Farrell expired, sometime in the first half of
1883, they moved to Kinigunan, about a mile
east of Kokopo, signed a contract with Herns-

23

[27] Mouton Senior to Monsieur Armand, 2 July 1885.

heim and were still trading for him when Mouton Senior died in 1888. During this time they were traders pure and simple; although they had bought some 5000 acres of land around Kinigunan, they did not think of emulating the example of Farrell, who started his first plantation at Ralum in 1883. Their only item of trade was coconuts; it was only later, after his father's death, that Octave started to diversify his trading activities. During most of the 1880s the pattern of trade still followed the indigenous one and the Moutons had little difficulty in fitting in. Possibly because they had little in common with most European residents, they did not keep themselves separate from the villagers. 'We have become accustomed to our new country,' wrote Mouton Senior in 1885, 'we are a bit like the natives and think little of tomorrow . . . In order to succeed one has to not only know their language but also find opportunities to participate in their ceremonies and I believe that no-one here is capable of doing that because most of them are frightened of the kanakas.'[27]

During their first year as traders the Moutons had one trading post, first at Ravalien and later at Kokopo. Soon after they started trading for Hernsheim, they had two: Mouton Senior remained at Kinigunan and Octave spent much of his time at Kabakaul. In 1886 they had five: the two already mentioned plus another three in nearby localities, following the current practice of leaving a small supply of goods with a trusted man in a village and calling back periodically to pick up the nuts he had bought. After his father's death Octave traded for the D.H.P.G. but became independent in 1894, with the financial backing of the Sacred Heart Mission. In the same year he started to diversify his

24

28 According to Blum 1900: 152, Mouton had a trading post on St John Islands in 1899. 29 Commonwealth Archives Office, CRS G2, F7 and CRS AA 63/83, box 65. Although Mouton had a European trader by the name of Duecker on the islands between 1909-12, his ships visited the group only irregularly, and the German administration was about to cancel his monopoly when the war broke out.

trading interests. He landed a profitable contract with the New Guinea Company to supply its Kokopo labourers with *taro* and also sold several shiploads of tortoise shell. In 1896-97 his boat made a number of trips to the Admiralty Islands to collect *bêche-de-mer* and to St John Islands to buy snail shells, but he failed to secure a permanent footing in either.[28] In 1897, together with Captain Rondahl, a Swede, and Captain Monrad, a Dane previously employed by Queen Emma, he formed the trading firm of Mouton and Co.

By the end of 1900, according to the *Annual Report of German New Guinea* for 1900-01, the firm employed two Europeans at Kinigunan, had a European trader at Balgai near Nusa, employed Chinese traders at Kabakaul, Gardner Islands and at Biritanai in northern New Ireland and 'stood in business relations' with independent European traders at Modip, Natava and Londip and with a native trader at Namalili (all on the Gazelle Peninsula); it also had 'business interests' on Kapinga-marangi and Ontong Java, the isolated outposts lying respectively south of the Carolines and north-east of the Solomons. In April 1903 Mouton brought off a real coup: he beat Hernsheim to a thirty years' concession granting him the monopoly of the copra trade on Kapingamarangi, in exchange for an undertaking to maintain a regular shipping service to the atolls, plus the payment of 500 marks annually.[29] The death of Monrad in September of the same year (Rondahl had left the partnership earlier) brought this expansion to a halt; if Mouton's experience with other masters, so well documented in the *Memoirs*, was at all typical, sober and hard-working captains were virtually impossible to find in New Guinea in those days. Still, in 1906 Mouton and Co. had twelve trading

[30] Imposed on all traders and artisans by an ordinance of 26 January 1905, the tax ranged from forty marks p.a. to 4000 marks, depending on the size of the concern. Copra plantations were not taxed because the export of copra was subject to an export levy (four marks a ton between 1888 and 1904, ten marks a ton after 1908).

[31] According to Salisbury 1970: 116, the Vunanami received 100 marks per ton of copra in 1896—an increase of some 300 per cent on 1882 prices.

posts in the Bismarck Archipelago—five more than the D.H.P.G., the same number as Hernsheim, and only four less than the New Guinea Company. In 1912 Mouton paid 2000 marks in business tax[30]—the same amount as the D.H.P.G., half the amount paid by Hernsheim and Co. and quarter the sum paid by Queen Emma's business successor, Rudolph Wahlen.

Thereafter Mouton gradually scaled down his trading activities, partly because of his age, no doubt, but mainly because he saw little prospect of success in competing with Burns, Philp and Co. (and later W. R. Carpenter and Co. Ltd as well) which had acquired a near-monopoly of the export-import trade by the end of the First World War. And he was the owner of a prosperous coconut plantation, in full bearing, which brought him a steady income without much exertion or undue worries.

Mouton's career as a plantation owner goes back to September 1891 when he planted the first ten hectares of his Kinigunan estate with coconut palms. He does not mention the reasons which prompted him to take the step at that particular time. Presumably the decision of the New Guinea Company to go ahead with large-scale planting around Kokopo was one such reason. The gradual increase in the price of coconuts[31] (and the growing tendency among villagers to make their own copra and sell it either green or sun-dried to the stations) which an astute businessman could only expect to continue, was probably another. Mouton's workforce consisted initially exclusively of locals. In spite of the Tolais' aversion to European style wage-labour he managed to recruit (the term is Mouton's) about a hundred villagers who stayed with him for about two years. It is on

[32] Parkinson 1887: 78.
[33] A coconut tree, under the cultivation methods prevalent in New Guinea before 1914, normally started bearing in its seventh year, with one hectare producing about 100 kg copra. The yield went up by 100 kg p.a. during the next two years, by 200 kg p.a. for the following three years, and reached 1000 kg in the thirteenth year. On good land (and Kinigunan was good land), under favourable conditions, one hectare yielded sometimes as much as 2000 kg p.a. (Preuss 1916: 542-43). The price of copra, in European ports, was as follows: £15-19 per ton in 1908, £18-23 in 1909, £21-28 in 1910, £21-28 in 1911, £24-28 in 1912, £22-33 in 1913 (Preuss: 541). In 1917-18 the f.o.b. price in Rabaul was £19, and two years later a phenomenal £33 per ton.

occasions like this that one wishes Mouton were more precise in his use of words. It seems likely that there was no *mekim pepa* on that occasion (if only because contracts were for three years and were rigidly enforced) and that Mouton, with his feeling for native ways, had preserved a sense of reciprocity in his relationship with the villagers. Clearing bush for gardens was traditionally a task where reciprocal work was normal and it may well be that this is how Mouton got most of his early clearing done. In return, he may have given them tobacco and possibly an occasional feast and a dance as his neighbour Parkinson had done so successfully on more than one occasion.[32] All this is, of course, conjecture. After the local villagers had left him, Mouton became his own recruiter: in 1892 he signed on a dozen labourers in Labur, in central-west New Ireland, in 1893 a group of thirty on Gardner Islands and in the following year a contingent from Bougainville. In 1901, he employed 157 labourers on his plantation and 286 two years later. This was reflected in the growth of the area under cultivation.

In 1895 Mouton had only forty-four hectares under coconut palms, as compared with 260 planted by the New Guinea Company at Kokopo and 400 by Queen Emma at Ralum. Three years later Mouton had about 350 hectares, as compared with the New Guinea Company's 750 and Queen Emma's 800. He did little new planting after 1900. From about 1904 onward, when most of his trees had begun bearing, he had a steady if unspectacular income from his plantation. After about 1911, when all his trees had reached maturity, his annual receipts from the sale of copra would never have been less than £6000, and perhaps twice as much in a year of bountiful crop and high prices.[33] To

27

[34] Blum 1900: 170. The minimum labour requirement was one worker per two hectares (Preuss 1916: 543).
[35] Overell 1923: 101.
[36] CAO, CRS 63/83, box 40, folder 5/96. Mouton lived with her as late as 1896 when, in a letter to Hahl, he had referred to her as 'ma femme canaque'.
[37] Ibid., box 44, folder 7 and 8/97.

arrive at his net income, we must deduct maintenance costs of about £7 per hectare per annum,[34] salaries of European staff, taxes, an export levy of ten shillings per ton of copra, and the occasional expenditure of a capital nature—say £3500 annually. This did not make Mouton a millionaire but it enabled him to invest wisely, to travel widely, and to live in a certain style. He spent almost a year in Europe in 1908-09 and again in 1919-20. When he happened to be up in New Guinea, his household included a much commented-on 'rarity, a governess from Sydney';[35] when he was down in Sydney his second wife had for a good many years a Vunanami *boi* and his *meri* to relieve her of the drudgery of household chores and to look after Mouton's younger son. He sold his plantation at a most opportune time, only a few months before the crash of 1929. His estate was worth £143,571 when he died in 1946.

For all his success, Mouton never quite made the grade with the local establishment— not that one gets the impression that he ever wanted to. He was probably too much of a solid *petit bourgeois* for the easy-going, here-today-gone-tomorrow assortment of traders and officials who met at the Kokopo hotel or the Rabaul Club. His appreciation of the 'kanaka ways' and in particular his 'marriage' to Yekanavo, a Nodup girl,[36] may also have influenced the attitude of the European community—though not necessarily so because Hahl, before he became Governor, also had a Tolai consort. Mouton's already-mentioned strained relations with Queen Emma—who for years was *the* local establishment—were not improved by his public attack (in 1896) on her past land acquisitions, which landed him in court on charges of defamation of character.[37] He also appears to have had some

[38] Ibid., Kaiserliches Bezirksgericht Herbertshoehe, folder 15/1906.
[39] Overell 1923: 163.
[40] I wish to record my warm appreciation of the generosity of Dr and Mrs Sturrock for allowing me access to the manuscripts and permitting their publication.

difficulty in controlling his temper, since on another occasion he found himself in court on charges of libel, after he had publicly 'insulted' one of Emma's employees[38]—although one should hasten to add that libel proceedings were a popular form of entertainment on the Gazelle Peninsula, providing as they did an exciting alternative to the 'monotony of afternoon teas and tennis'.[39]

Both the English and the French version of the *Memoirs* are in the possession of Mrs J. Sturrock of Mosman, New South Wales;[40] copies are held in the library of the University of Papua and New Guinea. As mentioned earlier, both versions are undated and they are unsigned. The French version chronicles events up to 1911 and is handwritten, while the English one is typed and has some marginal annotations. These are in a hand which is similar to Mouton's but is not his. The evidence for this statement can be found in one such annotation reproduced in footnote 77 which reads: 'Was given a piece of the boy but *says Octave* [italics supplied] I never ate it.' The handwriting is probably that of Mouton's third wife. We can visualise them going together through the *Memoirs* several years after they had been written, with Octave reminiscing and his wife making an occasional note. In that sense, Mouton can be regarded as the author of the marginal comments, if only because they mention facts with which only he himself could have been familiar.

The editing of the typescript presented a few minor problems. Since the quality of the typing was not all that could be desired, I decided initially to correct all obvious typing mistakes. It became soon apparent, however, that because of Mouton's educational background and life style some of these apparent mistakes were not mistakes at all. For instance, his inconsistency in the use of the plural and the past tense was almost certainly due to his superb command of Pidgin—even in his written English he occasionally slipped into Pidgin, as in 'the steamer belong the Marquis'. He also misspelt personal names, sometimes consistently, sometimes erratically (Van instead of Von Ortzen, Chambeaud instead of Chambaud, Schuller instead of Schulle) as well as place names, even of localities in Belgium. He was also inconsistent in his use of capitals, and his punctuation was haphazard. In spite of this I have tried to follow the original as closely as possible. Most of the 'obvious' typing mistakes have been left untouched, in particular those which reveal something of Mouton himself—for instance words like envie, enemie, unfaire and controle which betray his Gallic background. His capitals have not been interfered with and neither have his tenses, except on rare occasions. His singular has been changed into a plural only when matters of sense required it (as in 'Judge Tilmont and his son[s]', where Mouton obviously refers to all the judge's sons, or when the rest of the sentence made it necessary (as in 'the planters were those who were going to do the work, and make the colonial[s] wealthy, by cultivating the land for them'). Finally, all mistakes in the spelling of personal and place names, where the correct form could be ascertained, were corrected in the text itself, without recourse to footnotes.

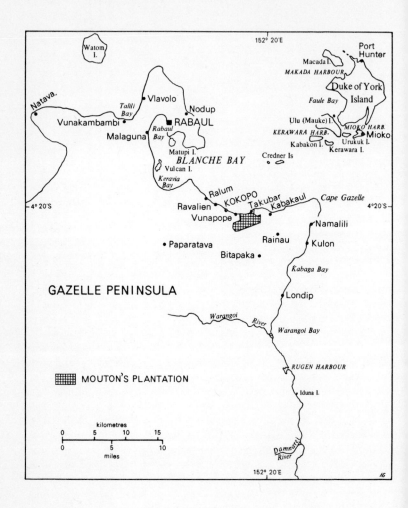

Watom I.

Natava.

Talili Bay

Vlavolo

Vunakambambi

Malaguna

Nodup

RABAUL

Rabaul Bay

Matupi I.

BLANCHE BAY

Vulcan I.

Keravia Bay

Ralum

Ravalien

KOKOPO

Takubar

Kabakaul

Cape Gazelle

Vunapope

Paparatava

Rainau

Bitapaka

Namalili

Kulon

152° 20'E

Macada I.

MAKADA HARBOUR

Port Hunter

Duke of York Island

Faule Bay

Ulu (Mauke) I.

KERAWARA HARB.

Kabakon I.

Kerawara I.

MIOKO HARB.

Mioko

Urukuk I.

Credner Is

4° 20'S

4°20'S

Kabaga Bay

Londip

Warangoi *River*

Warangoi Bay

RUGEN HARBOUR

Iduna I.

GAZELLE PENINSULA

▦ MOUTON'S PLANTATION

kilometres

0   5   10   15

0   5   10

miles

152° 20'E

Damna?el River

KG

The New Guinea Memoirs of Jean Baptiste Octave Mouton

I was born in Velaine Belgium, a small village between Namur and Charleroi, my parents were of small means, my father was a commercial traveller, as far as I know I understand that he was with the same Firm for thirteen years, Sapart was the name of this Firm. As far as I can remember I was more with my Grandmother than with my parents.

My first schooling was at Châtelineau, from there I went to Velaine with Grandmother, and attended school there, then I went to Nivelles also at school, this last school was under controle of Catholic Brothers, this is the last of my schooling, I was about eleven then. At that unfortunate early year I had to go to work and learn a trade and it was decided by my mother that coiffeur or barber was a good and easy trade, so I made my first apprentice as a barber at Nivelles. I stayed at Nivelles for about a year, then I shifted to Brussells. There I got into a barber shop but did not stay long at the first shop because I was doing only messages instead of learning then I got another job with a theatrical barber who did the La-Monaye works. This job was the happiest job of the lot, every night I could see the play from the top of the stage, our work as a rule was only needed after each act or change then we had to make a move, of course I did not do much only help in one way or other, the grown up men were doing the work, with this barber I had only to make wigs mostely with horse hair, and all the work were very rough material used for the making up of the artists.

33

Though I had a very good time there owing to the theatrical life, I was not satisfy with the work, I wanted to learn the trade properly late hours every night and rough work did not compensate for the opportunity of seeing the play, so I answered to an advertisement and got another job at the Passage St. Hubert, there all the best workmanship was done, I got the job and it is the job I wanted I was very keen to learn and there was a good opportunity with a master in the trade who was a Hollander, my earning was mighty small all I received was two franc fifty centime a week,[1] as apprentice the salary was very poor as the main point was to learn the trade.

In those days 1878 to 1880 time I was working, the trade was a trade and shaving was a secondary part of the trade, it was only after having served 3 years that an apprentice could go into salon as it is called, for shaving or doing ladies hair dressing, the workshop was the apprentice place, in those days Ladies has long hairs and were not satisfy with their own but had to add to it, le chignon était la mode, the chignon was the mode then and a great deal of false hairs were used, also we were making wigs for client for everyday wear, this work was very intriguing, the hair long plaits was done on three strong thread supported by two poles right and left of about three feet apart, the hair is then worked between those thread—then with the wig this is done on wooden heads, and the most difficult part is the parting which has to be on the left side or right or in the middle, and implanted one hair at a time and on hair tulle in such a way that it look quite natural, in my spare time I used to sneak some piece and work the parting, one day I was caught and I thought that I was going to get the sack, but on the contrary, the Boss was so surprised with my attempt and good finish, that if there was some very delicate wig to do he gave it to me to do it, of course he did not increase my small salary, but myself I was quite proud of it, at that time I was about 13 years old, and of course I was looked upon with envy by the others, they did not like me making such stride at all.

In 1880 there was the international exhibition at Brussells, my Boss was an exhibitor and was preparing his stall, and I had the

[1] About one shilling and sevenpence. The exchange rate for both the French and the Belgian franc was at that time twenty-five francs to one pound sterling.

good fortune to accompany him every time, so I was able to have a good look from the first start.

I remember all kind of industries, such as making felt, cutting diamond the mine where the diamond were found was represented in miniature, the niggers diggers and the whole working plant was represented, I remember that the polishing of the diamond was made by rubbing against diamond, the diamond was secured in a kind of strong wax or putty, and the men rubbed it against the other, the felt I remember consisted of a form in the shape of a bee hive, this revolved and the hairs which I understood was rabit hairs, were blown on it by a powerful machine, one blowed a liquid of very fine spray, and the other was the blower mentioned.

I also remember that there was an electric train and sundries, the plant was very crude, but it was electricity and the purpose was to show what it could be used for, the electricity usefulness was not yet acknowledged, the method now in vogue were not thought of, and for this reason the crude way of showing it was very interesting, it is very strange that those little episodes are quite clear in my mind, and I can see those stalls in my imagination, but I may not remember anything of recent happening, it seems to come and go and no notice is taken by my brain.

It was at that periode of my life that, my Father become acquinted with a Mr. Schurman an Hollander, who represented some American firm for agriculture implement such as shovel forks etc, whatever it was he did not make anything by it, and he was living from mouth [hand] to mouth, he appeared of a very intelligent man, I understand that he had some experience with the Dutch colonie, in fact I was told by my father that he was born in Sarang,[2] he could speak malay like a native, he also had a small knowledge of Chinese.

This Schurman become acquainted with the Marquis de Rays expedition to colonize in a part called New France (Nouvelle France), and called the Colonie Libre de Port Breton, and he made arrangement with the representative Dr de Groote[3] who

[2] This is almost certainly a spelling mistake. Mouton seems to refer either to Serang (West Java), or, more likely, to Samarang (Central Java). He uses the latter on p. 43.

[3] A retired naval doctor, P. de Groote was the Consul of New France for Belgium and the Marquis' propagandist-in-chief. His *Nouvelle-France: Colonie*

was in Brussells doing the propaganda, there was a newspaper called 'La Nouvelle France', this paper represented the new enterprise as a wonderful thing, picture showing, sceneries of unimaginable prospects, of course those sceneries were taken from quite a different part of the world, but we did not know, however, as we had nothing to lose and all to win, my father was quite taken with the prospect, and as far I can remember the conditions were as follow or rather the prospect.

The Marquis de Rays sold land in the Nouvelle France to whom may buy it at the rate of 5 Francs an hectare (or 2½ acres) the land would be cultivated by colonial workers[4] and the profit would be distributed amongst the shareowners, or rather in this case by the landowners. Those who were as colonials to cultivate the land for the benefit of the landowner, were to be alloted with so many hectare of land, with the exception that they were kept at the expense of enterprise there was no wages stipulated, I think that my Father was under the Colonial, that is the man under Schurman to cultivate the million of hectares of land for the owners, that was our understanding and father did not know better than what he was told. Mr. Sapart the leather manufacturer having died suddenly while walking in the street, the whole business went to pot, and to get another job was very hard, so

---

Libre de Port-Breton, which appeared in October 1880 (well after the *Chandernagor* disaster mentioned in fn. 19), described the colony in most glowing terms and held out totally unrealistic prospects for potential settlers; it also claimed that the Marquis himself visited New Ireland although he had never done so.

[4] Elsewhere Mouton uses the term planters, but both names are misleading, since the individuals he has in mind were called *ouvriers agricoles* (agricultural labourers). These 'colonial workers' were indentured for five years, during which period they were to be entitled to free board and lodgings but received no cash wages except a vaguely defined share in profits, depending on their 'conduct and labour'. After five years they were to be given a house and twenty hectares of 'good' land. Passage to Port-Breton was not free; a single worker had to pay 500 francs, and a family 1200 francs, irrespective of size. The 'colonial workers' should not be confused with the 'colonials' mentioned by Mouton in the next sentence of the text. The latter were officially called *émigrants-colons*, paid a minimum of 3000 francs per family (or per 'association of four persons'), and were entitled to '3rd class passage', a four-room house, twenty hectares of land and free rations for six months. Many *colons* on the *Nouvelle Bretagne* had invested considerably more than the minimum. Mouton Senior was an agricultural labourer.

he accepted with the vision of making good, not having any knowledge of tropical life or the way of things relied on his friend Schurman to see to it, he did not care where the wind blowed, it was better than stay in Belgium with no prospect ahead.

Therefore on a September cold night in 1880 my father and myself left Brussells at 11 p.m. left the Gare du Nord accompnied with a young Hollander named Hulster, arrived at Paris at about 4 a.m. at this early hour all we could see is the people going to market for the daily supply of Paris, in those days there was no restaurants train, and at our arrival after a very cold night travel we felt very peckish, so we bought bread one botle claret and some fromage de Brie, and to this day I think that it was the best meal I ever had to taste so good, we partaked of this in our room, after securing a moderate hotel.

At Paris we expected to see Schurman, the notary Chambaud and three other young men, H. Hauterman, André, and Jule, two of those young men were realy black sheep of this family, I understood that the Father send them away to better themselve and get out of the way, we stayed in Paris one day.

Then we left Paris for Havre our destination so far, where we were to continue our trip by the steamer 'Nouvelle Bretagne' a wood ship steamer of about 2000 tons, build in Norway,[5] after we were properly installed, the next day we went and interviewed the Marquis who was installed in a very poor lodging, for a man of his importance, he then informed us that the French Government objected to take more than 39 passengers on board, but we were to remain at Havre until further orders, we were then in a moderate boarding house near the wharf, the food was very good and to this day I still think that it was the best meal we ever had, just good plain French good cooking, we stayed at Havre for quite a long time I think at least two months, we had nothing to do but taking it easy, during all those days we only saw Schurman twice he prefered to stay at Paris, some of the other members of the expedition were installed in an other large boarding house, but we never met them very much.

---

[5] Originally the *Ingebord*, bought by the Marquis for 135,000 francs. It was much smaller than asserted here; in the French version (p. 6) Mouton says that it was 'no bigger than 400 tons'. It was eventually sold for a pittance in Manila and the proceeds were used to pay off the crew.

After the 'Nouvelle Bretagne' left Havre with the only passengers allowed, we also left Havre for Barcelona Spain to join the steamer, we were in all three myself Father and Hulster a young Hollander, the rest went their own way.

We passed again Paris but stayed there three days, we met Schurman and Chambaud who was to be a Notary at Port Breton, those people were then staying at Paris, we also met the Hauterman André, Jule, and Henry, André knew Paris very well and those three days were well filled to see the sight, unfortunately we could only do it cheaply, our finance were very low, Schurman did not give father much to go on with, however our stay at Paris was too short.

Here end our stay at Paris and we are on the move for Barcelona, the three of us, Schurman was to follow with the rest that is the Hauterman brothers. We managed to find a moderate lodging near the quay, not so good as at Le Havre, but we had nothing to complain about, the food was spanish cooking, which use much garlic and everything is mixed with red powder, after a week or so we got used to it, at the same lodging there were also a French family, consisting of father mother two sons and a daughter, the boys were of my age, so we had a very good time while at Barcelona, having nothing to do but kill time, we only came back for our meals, I remember that there was hardly a day we did not come to trouble with spanish boys, who seemed to have a grudge agains us French, there was not a day that did not finish with some battle of some sort,[6] fortunately for us boys there was a boy who spoke french who took fancy to me we were great friends, but had no time for the other boys, I do not know why, through him I learned spanish and could make myself understood which was a great help to me, unfortunately having no practice I lost it, or rather not enough foundation to have the language rooted into my brain, I was rather quick in learning language, in fact as I see things now and what I had to go through, if I had the chance I would have done better than my sons now.

We stayed at Barcelona at least three months as I did not keep a diary it is hard to remember the proper length of time but I

[6] One of the reasons for this lack of cordial relations might have been the fact that 'for three months one could see in the streets of Barcelona young men in strange uniforms'—a reference to the Port-Breton militia (Lucas-Dubreton 1929: 7-8).

know that it was not less than three months, it seemed to me that there was trouble about leaving Europe, this of course I was too young to worry about or take notice, and the great drawback was that my education was not good enough to do it.

There were about 120 emigrants including soldiers and colonials,[7] the soldiers were to guard the peace and protect the settlers, the settlers were those who bought land at five francs per hectare or five francs for two and half acre, and the planters were those who were going to do the work,[8] and make the colonials wealthy, by cultivating the land for them, but the workers were to be compensated by land for their work, the whole expedition comprising of all nation, there were French, Belgium, Spaniard, Italian, German, I do not remember of any Englishmen, I and father were amongst the planters under Schurman who was in charge of the planters, with the exception of the military lot who had more officers than men, the majority were of the poor land owners and called colonial, and we were only the part to cultivate the land.

The French Government seemed to make objection to the expedition, and even Spanish, however when the 'Nouvelle Bretagne' was ready to leave Barcelona that is after about three months wasting time for which I did not know the reason, but no doubt it was owing to Government objection, at the last moment when the ship was ready many of those people who took advantage of being kept for all this time left at the last moment, and only a half of the expedition shipped on board the 'Nouvelle Bretagne', the rest deserted with the protection of Government, and I may say that it was a good job, because if the full complement had shipped I do not know where they could have been accommodated on board the ship, as we were like sardines, amongst those who deserted two of the Hauterman André and Jule the only one who went was Henry the best son of the lot, it would have been very bad for us had we had bad weather, packed like sardines as we were, however we did not do too bad of course compared with the present it was rather rough but we did not think so, at least I didnt, I never was sea sick for one thing, which mean a lot, every thing

---

[7] Actually 150 (Hueskes 1932: 20; Stephan 1905: 331; Robson 1965: 226). Note also the French version: 'There were many emigrants on board some 120 to 200 people colons and soldiers of all nations' (p. 7).

[8] See fn. 4.

was new to me, and I made the best of it, knowing what privation is.

Our first stopping port was Port Said, there I first came in contact with strange peoples and hot climate, a mixture of races Arab amongst them as predominant, we coaled there and it took three days to do it, during day time we went on shore and saw the town, at night we went on board again, this enable us to see the most of the town, the bazar and all the strange way of the people were very interesting to me. Having our full load of coal we started on the forth day to go through the Suez channel, we stopped at night and anchored near the bank, no vessel could go at night, on one occasion we had to make room for an English transport, who carried troup to Africa for the Zoolou war I think, or the Sudan I forgot which,[9] all I know is that was fearfully hot not a breath of wind, it was a very trying passage, and it took us four or five days before we reached Suez and so on through the Red Sea, nothing special only we had an Arab pilot on board who would not partake of our food he made his own cooking which was very simple but to me it was strange, the only excitement was that we saw several large sharks who were following the ship monsters they were.

Our next stop was Aden, a very barren country there was no green to be seen, we stayed at an Hotel with Schurman, Henry, father and self also Chambaud with his wife, I forgot to mention that Hulster did not come with us he left us at Barcelona, at Aden we stayed at the hotel for three days, I remember that the mosquitos were terrible it was the first time I felt them, at the back of the hotel were we stayed there was a big heap of bones, and probably was the cause for the mosquitos the weather was very dry and trying for us coming from Europe, when we were there they said that it did not rain for seven years, perhaps I made a mistake it may be seven months, at any rate we were drinking distilled water from sea water, this big heap of bone must have been for some industrie of some sort, what it was for I do not know, but it was a very large one, I did not like Aden at all nothing much to see there.

Our next stop was Ceylon Point Galle or Gala Point, this was an eye opening to me, the vegetation was wonderful all tropical fruits to be had were there, the country was wonderful and green,

[9] The Sudan War: the Zulu campaign was over by 1881.

this was the first glance at the real tropical vegetation, we stayed at an hotel for three or four days, the stay was too short for me because for the first time there was such a great contrast with the other places and above all Aden, the climat was also very bearable every surounding being so green the heat was cooled by it, and very soothing to the eye, it was the first time I tasted banana and pineapple, so you can imagine, not having tasted banana or pineapple and mangoes in my life though I have seen them in Brussells for sale, I could not aford the luxury, I had to be content with the smell of it. I remember that in the arcade in Brussells was a greengrocer who sold all kind of expensive fruits such as those mentioned, many time I tought that I would like to taste them, the smell was so enticing.

Our next stop was Singapore, making our fourth stop since leaving Barcelona, I liked Singapore very much, it was far more busy than Ceylon and there was a great number of Chinese, and the shipping made this port more lively.

We rented a two storey house and cooked our own food, which was not very satisfactory, for the simple reason the cook expert was missing. However this only lasted a few days then we got our suply from the convent, the Sisters were kind enough to supply us twice a day lunch and dinner, breakfast we cooked ourselves in the continental fashion coffee and bread and butter, that is all we required as we were used to it. At lunch time a Chinaman would bring in on his shoulder hanging on a bamboo stick, two sets of enameled plate or dishes containing our meal, at every meal there was curry as in Singapore there was no meal without curry, the curry act as an ordeuvre, at night the Chinaman did the same, all I had to do was wash up, and the next day the carrier would take the one he left in the morning and leave the one he brought and so on, having two sets in use.

In this house we were in all six peoples, Schurman, Judge Tilmont[10] his sons and daughters, and father and myself.

The water for our bath was brought by a chinaman who charged a few cents for it, our bath consisted of large wooden tub, this was

[10] He was, to use Mouton's terminology, a 'colonial' (*émigrant-colon*) who was said to have invested his entire fortune of 25,000 francs in the venture. He and his six children were stricken by malaria soon after arrival; the whole family was eventually evacuated to Manila on the *Nouvelle Bretagne* (see fn. 33).

filled and with a dip made of cocosnuts shell fastened to a stick as handle this acted as a shower, the method being to pour over the body with a laddle, I must say that we found the bath very nice and cool, having our supply as mentioned before, we had plenty time on hand, the house did not take much trouble as there was no furniture except chair bed and table, and our crockery, and the usual wash stand, no wardrobe our cloths were hanged on the wall with a kind of printed material cover. I used to go about on my own, I soon become friendly with a boy who lived next door, he could talk a little French so I learned Pigin English for the first time, at that time the only language I could master was French, it was not very long before I could quite use the Pigin English, and this become very useful later.[11]

My only trouble then was with Miss Tilmont she was a pest, she was a great cigarette smoker, and never put a hand to anything in way of help she was the most useless person I ever met, I do not know that she was useless or that she did not want to do anything, for all I know is that she did not make her own cigarettes even, that is if she saw me handy, she asked me to make her cigarettes for her, and as she smoked a great deal I was sometime very busy at it, I was I may say through her great demand quite an expert in making cigarettes, not only that but she was a great nuisance, if she wanted anything on the table near enough for her to reach, she would ask anyone near to pass it to her. At the end it got upon my nerves; if I had any in those days I dont think, but at last I could not stand it more and I stood my own ground and dodged her when the opportunity arised, and had all kind of excuse to get away from her, she could do nothing against that because she had no controle over me in any shape or form, what I did first was to be agreable to her, until it became an abuse then I had to kick,

---

[11] It is a pity that Mouton did not elaborate this point, in view of the still unresolved question of the origin of Melanesian Pidgin (see, for instance, the conflicting views expressed in Wurm 1966 and Salisbury 1967). What he seems to be saying is that in the early 1880s there was little difference between the Singapore Pidgin and that used in the Bismarck Archipelago—an impression which is strengthened by his references to *demi-Anglais* or *Anglais bâtard* in the French version. One of the main difficulties here stems from the fact that virtually all recorded samples of early Melanesian Pidgin come from individuals who spoke or at least understood English. Since Mouton did neither when he arrived in New Guinea, anything he might have said on the subject would have been of great interest to linguists and social historians.

and I had to be rude and tell her the strength of her tyrany and in plain speaking I told her what I tought of her, she did not like it and make a great fuss by crying and complaining about my insolence etc. I did not care I wanted to get free from her and I did, do not make a mistake I was only fourteen years of age only a boy, and wanted as much time to myself as I could, so that I could go out with my friend, even if she went out she wanted me to go with her, I could see only one thing and that she intended to make a slave of me so I had to act and be rude. We stayed at Singapore rather a long time, what was the reason I do not know, and it must have cost something to keep the whole expedition because beside us there was the others who were in a kind of boarding house in town, where we were we had the luck to be out of town proper and in a secluded part of the town, which was very agreable, nevertheless it did not worry me and I was too young to know the why and wherefore, but no doubt it must have been financial matter, at Singapore we had a very large supply of all kind, which had to be paid for so I think that it was the reason, Schurman bought all kind of plants in specially made cases, coffee, nutmeg, etc., all what he thought would be needed as a start, but now when I think of it, what a fleabite it was to cope with the vast enterprise the expedition aim was, Schurman was the only member of the expedition who knew something about tropical plants, I understand that he was born at Samarang of Dutch parents, he spoke malay fluently, and chinese a bit, he could speak five languages, and very fluently as well, and I am sure with his knowledge, had he had any sort of inducement and the soil and labour to work with he was a very capable man and would have been very valuable in a plantation.

I think our stay at Singapore must have lasted at least three months and during that time other passengers deserted but not so many as in Barcelona, it appear that there was some sort of rumours about the object aim of the expedition, and no doubt they were well earned.

At Singapore a sailing barque was added to our equipment, she was an old vessel three masted barque, renamed 'Marquis de Rays'[12] the cargo as well as member of the expedition were divided between the 'Nouvelle Bretagne' and the 'Marquis de Rays' and

[12] Originally the *Nettie Merriman*. She was bought by Captain Henry for 25,000 francs and was used as a hospital ship in Port-Breton.

43

we were some of them but Schurman and the other crowd of our party remained on the steamer. There was no cabin accommodation, our sleeping gears were hammocks hanging on the beam of the ship under the first hole of the ship, when the hatch could be left open it was not too bad but God help when bad weather it was unbearable, with the exception of the sleeping part of it, the deck was very pleasant we had plenty space to move about which we did not get on the 'Nouvelle Bretagne'.

But before continuing I must relate the incident of my trouble on shipping; we chartered a large sampan to load our belonging which consisted of our luggages and poultry etc. me and my father were in charge of the sampan, think were going nicely when to our surprise we saw our ship leaving her anchorage and moving toward the entrance of the harbour, and to try to reach her with this big sampan was too slow so my father got a smaller sampan and followed making sign, but to my horror the boat continued and took no notice of my father signal and there I was left alone in charge of this sampan with malays. Then my trouble began with the malays they refused to go further, and the only way left was to go back to the wharf, the malays started to take things from the cargo and showed nasty, it was out of the question to make them follow the vessel, in my ignorance of the movement of the vessel I thought it was just as well to go on shore and find out, so I told the malays to make for the Agent wharf, but they did not they landed in fair distance from the wharf I wanted them to land, so I demonstrated with them that they were not acting according to my instructions, and I made them understand that I was going to the Agent, some of them tried to stop me but I threatened them with the call for the police, they let me go, this threat seemed to have cooled them a bit, so I reached the Agent and explained matters, as I reached the Agent to my great relief I met some of the members and they told me that the boat would be at anchore for another two days, so there was plenty time to reach the boat with the cargo the same day before dark, but as the distance was further the malays wanted more pay, and tried to take advantage of my inexperience, when I explained to the Agent they were a bad lot and that they had poached the cargo, of course this made a different construction to their claim, for their pilfering made them guilty and lost their right to claim more, so they had to take the price of the first contract and say nothing, of course all pilfered goods were returned.

44

With a crew finding themselve outwitted I came on board the ship at about four o'clock in the afternoon, the distance really was no more than double a matter of a few hours only, when I arrived I found my father on board and everybody having a good laugh at me and called me Captain au long cour, which mean deep sea Captain, well I did not think so, when I come to think of it my father could have taken steps to let me know as soon as he knew, of course he did not think that I would have trouble with the malays and that they keep going like they did, well I suppose when he saw that there was plenty of time that I would follow and did not think of the treachery of the malays, the trouble was that the malays pilfered a case of brandy and started to drink it, it appear that it was the only thing that they were afraid of, and they asked me if I did not say anything about it they would cause no trouble any more and that the cargo with me would be delivered in no time, I kept that promise the only thing they lost was a large fee, and we left the best of friends, amongst the crew there was only one who could speak English, or rather Pigin English.

All these anxieties would have been avoided if Schurman had informed father, and I was kept going with the joke of deep sea Captain. To continue we are on board the 'Marquis de Rays' and waiting for the departure she is loading explosive by what I am told, and now continue our life on board.

The 'Marquis de Rays' being an old barque was towed by the 'Nouvelle Bretagne' so our progress was not very fast, and our worst time was at night, the vessel having been at anchore for some time, was full of vermins, cockroaches and centipede scorpions were very bad, especially cockroaches flying all over the ship, and it was not a surprise to see one having his toes or sole of his feet nipped during the night.

The Captain of the ship was a young Norwegian,[13] a rather decent fellow with the exception of night we were not so bad during daytime we had our work, cleaning and cooking was on the program, there was no special crew to do it.

After a little while we got used to it and by hunting the vermins it was more bearable the first week was horrible, fortunately we had good weather the most part of the trip, if we had had bad weather I do not know how we would have stood it.

---

[13] Captain Bull, formerly an officer on the *Nouvelle Bretagne*.

45

Our course was along the coast of Sumatra at the time we could see gunsmoke on the shore where the Dutch were fighting with the natives,[14] our next stop was Sangire[15] an Island in the Celebes, this Island was occupied by a Dutch Missionar who had a very nice nutmeg plantation, of which he received a nice income. We took water and also nutmeg plants. Schurman managed to get them from him, no doubt Schurman was a wonder he could rattle malay like a malay, and no Chinaman could get the best of him in any bargaining. We stayed at that Island a few days. We kept going along all the Islands and our next sixth stop was on the coast of New Guinea, an Island called Arimoa on the chart there may be another name[16] but it was the name the Captain gave us. We had to get water, we anchored into a little harbour the Island looked very attractive but there was no sign of life at first, but later one canoe showed nearby but not too close, it was evident that the natives were not used to whiteman, but must have had some dealing with some sort of peoples bartening with them, those people were well build and had a bow and arrow, naked with only a small covering made of bark of some sort, dark skin more like malay type color than the papuan type, they were very shy at first and it took some time before one more daring than the others came on board, and Captain Henry who had his wife aboard made soon friendly term with him, he was shown the cabin of the 'Nouvelle Bretagne' and presents were made, and what surprised him most was Mrs Henry playing the piano, it seem to me that Mrs Henry was the principal instrument of peace maker.

After that when this native went on shore a score of canoes came to the ship and in no time the next day we were surrounded with canoes bringing fruits and turtle shells, to exchange with trade the only ones who did a good business were the Malays we had on board, they knew the value of turtle shells and they bought all they

[14] Another slip of memory: after leaving Singapore, the expedition steamed along the north coast of Borneo (Baudouin 1885: 102). Mouton himself says in the French version (p. 12): 'Having left Singapore we went past Borneo and from the ship we could see the smoke of the Dutch cannons as they fought 'les Atchinois' (Atjeh?).

[15] I.e. Sangihe, an island about 150 miles north of Manado.

[16] Actually a group of three islands off the northern coast of West Irian (c. 1°35′S, 138°50′E)—Niru Moar, Lansutu and Liki. Malay traders, who frequented them regularly, called them Kumamba Islands (Wichmann 1909: 69).

could with small cheap pocket knives, we europeans did not know only one here and there took notice and bought it only to make ornament with it, this prove that it was not the first time they did business in that line with white or Malay, those natives brought quite a large quantity of turtle shell and very good quality at that, but we poor fools did not know and with the exception of one or two more clever the Malays had the best of it, those malays where part of the fishing gang to fish for the residents of the colonie to come.

They also brought cocos nuts, banana, taro, yams and sundry tropical fruits and vegetable, taros and yams were unknown to us the only ones who used them was the malays again who cooked them as food.

The first attempt to get water was a failure, on arrival no sooner we dropped anchore the Captain send a boat on shore to get water but they had to come back without it, the natives did not look too promising, but after the peace was made and they knew that we were friendly there was no trouble and they helped to get the water, it is fortunate that there was no need at the first instance to exchange shot and kill some of the natives, we would have had water all right but by force a landing party would have made short work with the natives. As it was it was possible for us to go on shore and have a good look and strech our legs, everything was new to us, it was the first meeting with real savages man eaters and head hunters.

After we had all the water we needed and firewood for cooking to save the coal we left Arimoa just as we were very friendly with the natives, now we are on our way to the land of Paradise and our goal. Jogging along at the tail of the 'Nouvelle Bretagne' until a day came that if we kept going as we did we would be short of coal, and in such predicament there would be no reaching the promised land, so it was decided that the steamer would go ahead and leave us to sail the rest of the voyage,[17] and then sailors were

---

[17] If we accept Baudouin's version of the incident (1885: 104-05), the separation of the two ships was not the outcome of a 'decision'—it simply happened. It seems that the quarter-master of the *Nouvelle Bretagne*, unhappy about the overstraining of the engine of 'his' ship, cut one of the strands of the rope which linked the *Marquis de Rays* with the steamer. About an hour later the rope broke and the two ships began to part company. After waiting all night for the *Marquis de Rays* to catch up with his ship, Captain Henry decided to

put on board the barque and we sailed on our own power for the first time, while Captain Henry went ahead with the 'Nouvelle Bretagne' to meet again later at the end of our voyage unless she could find coal enough to pick us again but this was not the case and we had to keep going the best we could the vessel being very old the Captain did not trust the masts, and at the slightest strong breeze which would have been a good sailing breeze he had to shorten sails, of course this did not help us a bit.

The Captain knew his work all right he was a very good sailor, and worked the ship well to the capacity of the gears he had to handle. So now we are on our own, I do not know our exact position, but we must be close to our destination, because we had the South east wind which was against us, and the boat had to tack our way through. I think that we must have been more than one week doing this, wind and current against us and a slow vessel, slow because we could not carry sails, I thought that we never would reach the place.

However, after a long tedious time we managed to reach Port Hunter in Duke of York Island only a few miles from our goal.[18] We stayed about a week at Port Hunter, this Port Hunter was occupied by the Methodist Mission, and while we were there our people put a monument made of coral stone on the graves of the 11 or 12 of the former members of a previous expedition who died and were buried on the Island,[19] the story go that they all died

---

proceed to Port-Breton alone, since the *Nouvelle Bretagne* had hardly any coal left. According to Baudouin, the ships became separated 'at the entrance to St. George's Channel, or more precisely, at the latitute of Elisabeth Island' (also known as Alim Island and located south of the Admiralty Islands). The *Nouvelle Bretagne* arrived at Port-Breton on 10 July and the *Marquis de Rays* five weeks later.

[18] Note the corresponding passage in the French version: 'The *Génil* came to our rescue . . . and finally towed us to Port Hunter in the Duke of York Islands . . . After a few days the wind abated, the *Génil* returned [from Port-Breton] and towed us to our destination.' (p. 13).

[19] The dead belonged to the *Chandernagor* contingent and were among the forty-two men evacuated from Liki-Liki by the Methodist missionaries on 2 April 1880 (Brown 1908: 353-70). Brown mentions that eight evacuees died at the mission headquarters but was unable to account for four of the forty-two men rescued, so that Mouton's figure is probably correct. Most of the survivors from the *Chandernagor* sailed for Sydney on 1 September 1880 on the *Victor*. Among those who remained as traders were the following: Tetzlaff, Semeriva,

of malaria fever, and I quite believe if they were lacking of quinin as we were, this Island was beautiful and while we were there we went on shore every day, the natives seemed to be very peaceful, I presume that the Mission had a great deal to do with it, though they were only begining to teach their Gospel. After a week about the 'Génil' a small steamer belong the Marquis de Rays came at last to our rescue and towed us to Port Breton it took only a few hours to do that.

We arrive at Port Breton on the 15th of August 1881 at 4 p.m. and what a delusion, our paradise become a hell rather than a land of promise, some of the passengers were so much affected that they cried of disappointment, imagine coming into a small harbour which was no more than a little bay which could only hold about three vessels a fourth one would be an impossibility, the vessel could not swing round her anchore without coming in collision with the other, this small hole to make matter far more ugly was surrounded by high mountains reaching the clouds the summit was covered by cloud, at the time of our entrance into the Port there was no cloud to be seen, only rain and such rain, this rain lasted at least forty eight hours, before it cleared, then we were able to see what we came to.

The more accurate explanation to this hole is that it represented a funnel such as used to fill bottles the bottom was the little bit of land I should say no more than 100 acres at the end of which the hill rised very steep right up the sky, climbing was very difficult owing to the steepness, we saw some few buildings there along the shore which were only sheds and the rest heavy timbered land rising to the sky, owing to the rain it was not too hot, and our vision was not too good either owing to the same reason.

According to the description given by the Marquis de Rays newspaper the Colonie Libre de Port Breton was much to be desired this newspaper called 'La Nouvelle France' made a paradise of this hell of a land, and for this reason we felt it much more,

---

Lemesle (or Lemele), Benninger, Coulfuty (or Coulfitie), Brandt and Coenen (by the time the Moutons landed in Mioko, in February 1882, Benninger had been killed by the villagers and Coulfuty had committed suicide). Not a single emigrant from the *India* settled in New Guinea and only three members of the *Nouvelle Bretagne* expedition were to do so: the Moutons and a Frenchman called Dupré. By 1900 only Mouton, Coenen and Lemesle were still in New Guinea and in 1909 only Mouton and Lemesle remained.

we came to the two extremes. No doubt this newspaper got those pictures and informations from other countries[20] and made use of it for his own paper to deceive the poor fools who spend their saving to buy land, those were indeed to be pitied, and one of them named Pitoy[21] was nearly out of his head when he asked where shall find my 1800 hectares, there he was pulling his hair and crying the poor devil was to be pitied.

Well now after anchore touched bottom we met Schurman who was wearing an oilskin coat, he did not look too happy, and Henry Hauterman was not better either both looked very much on the gum, no doubt Schurman realised the deceiving part of the whole enterprise, there his knowledge and experience were not to be of any value, his disappointment must have been terrible.

I will try to describe this famous Port Breton, to the best of my ability. The Harbour look very small and is no more than a little bay protected by the narrow entrance and a reef with room enough for about two or three vessels and not too large at that, along the harbour there was a road made by the members of the previous emigrants, this road was about 12 feet wide, the far side of the bay was occupied by the main body a long building like a shed without ornament but more like a long shed made of corrugated iron roof and walls, this long shed called block-house had for walls weatherboard, the whole construction was divided into sections, I may say of about 14 to 16 feet wide to the depth of the shed, in this lived a lot of people, but I remember well that at one end was the part used for the Church, then came the

---

[20] Most of the illustrations came from the seventy-volume publication called *L'Univers: Histoire et Description de tous les Peuples* (Paris, 1835-63), popularly known as *L'Univers Pittoresque*. On the skilful use of illustrations by the Marquis and his associates in general, see Baudouin (1885: 72-74).

[21] A typical *émigrant-colon*, Auguste Eustace Pitoy came from the Lorraine and was a fairly prosperous barge-owner before he decided to emigrate with his wife, three children and a niece. During the sea-voyage 'he spent his days dreaming about his life at Port-Breton. His house would give to the east, and would be surrounded by a huge orchard ... My property, he would say [studying the map] will be called *Nancy*. This little river which runs through it, I shall name the *Moselle*. And this mountain here I shall name the *Montagne Thiers*, in honour of the liberator of France' (Baudouin 1885: 92). Both Pitoy and his wife died at Port-Breton: the children and the niece grew up in Australia and their descendants are still alive in New South Wales.

different families and even Italians had some of the partition alloted to them, there was also a few other building of the same pattern and made of native material no doubt made by the new arrivals for freedom of space, in those building there were the Priest[22] who made use of the church for a sleeping room as well, the officers and their wives, Colons with their families, Italians and Spaniards, soldiers of all nations, in all I presume that the whole colonie upon this little space of land was about say 60 or 70 if that much, all living according to who they were in those departments.

Along the bay a little farther about say 600 yards was a cottage, which must have been build for the former Governor,[23] this cottage was occupied by the Notary Chambaud with his wife and child, this was the best of the lot as far as architecture is concerned, the ground available for cultivation was very poor it consisted of a flat of no more the 100 acres if that much with a river going through this water came from the hill and in reality was only an outlet the width was no more than 100 feet the water was like chrystal so pure and clear that is the best part of the whole setlement, on this flat the settlers had made some attempts to gardening and there was indication that the former settlers had done the same because the land was cleared and what the present ones had to do was to clear the small growth and it was ready for gardening, I think that this was the only thing this land could be used for there was not enough to do anything with it, beside should the river overflow what would happen, God know. There was also the remain of the last expedition, part of

[22] Abbé René-Marie Lanuzel. Born in 1846, he was a captain of a Breton contingent in the Franco-Prussian war, became a priest in 1874 and was a secular missionary in Haiti until 1879. Although he went to Port-Breton at the behest of the Sacred Congregation for the Propagation of Faith, he was not officially a missionary; Rome, at this stage, 'supplied a priest, but with its customary prudence, was not involved in the adventure itself' (Dupeyrat 1935: 39). He came out on the *India*, accompanied Rabardy and le Prevost to Sydney and returned on the *Génil* in February 1881. He then acquired a piece of land near Nodup in a locality referred to by Jouet as Beridni and by Hueskes as Matanakunai but his house was burned down by the villagers after a few months. He returned to Europe in October 1881 and was later sent to New Zealand. He did not return in 1883 as claimed in Salisbury (1970: 27) nor did he die in Rabaul as stated in Niau (1936: 78).

[23] Colonel J. A. le Prévost.

sugar machinery, it appear that the machinery arrived before the sugar cane could be planted, or even find enough land to plant I am sure that it could not be done at Port Breton.

We were in a way more fortunate, our selected part was about 5 miles farther along the coast in a bay called Bay Marie,[24] this bay was very exposed and could not be used as shelter for anchorage, the place was also a flat surrounded by high mountains, but we were more open, there was building build by the first settlers, this building was build of logs and of two stories, ceiling also build of logs, on the wall there was loopholes for the insertion of guns, like a barrack it seems to me that thoses peoples were prepared for an attack if it should occure, we all lived there for the time being, then we build a shed made of malay mats which we brought from Singapore with us, this was very soon made, when the frame was up the rest was simple we had only to nail the mats on the frame, this shed was about 40 feet long by 12 feet wide, and about 7 feet high, at one end the cooking place which was very simple, and our dining room, then all the rest was used for sleeping, our floor was the earth, and our bed iron one at that was simply on it.

While Father Schurman and Henry Hauterman and myself lived in this shed the Judge Tilmont and his sons and daughters were living in the log house, our time was filled with making a fowl house for our poultry platforms for our plants, clearing the land available which was no more than 50 acres if that much, as far as I can remember the only thing growing was pumkin and water melons,[25] there was no proper soil for anything else, my part of the business was to kill time by cooking and sometime do

[24] Also called Port St Joseph by the settlers and known today as Irish Cove. The main settlement was at the Baie Française (or Port des Français)—today's English Cove. The distance between the two settlements was actually two and a half miles; in the French version (p. 15) Mouton says it took him about an hour to cover it.

[25] Octave's pumpkins drew an appreciative comment from J. Poulain who visited both Baie Marie and the main settlement six months after the final evacuation (see fn. 39). 'What passion the settlers must have had for pumpkin,' said the Director of the Societé des Fermiers-Généraux de la Nouvelle-France, but otherwise gave them full marks: 'They tried hard to grow things here, much harder than at Port-Breton' (Poulain 1883: 99). Poulain was tried at the same time as the Marquis and sentenced to five years' imprisonment.

some clearing, and sometime fishing with the natives when I could spare the time.

From the Bay Marie where we were the first settlers made a road to the main settlement Port Breton, I should think of about five miles long, this road we used when the sea was too bad, when the weather was favorable we used a native made canoe, which was made of a hollow wood with an outrigger this canoe would hold about four peoples, but generally it was my job to go to Port Breton to get the ration twice a week, this consisted of wine claret, salt pork, coffee, rice, and olive oil, and biscuits, unfortunately flour was not used, and butter was unknown, and only those who knew better had a better diet, for instance we had condensed milk and a little butter in tin which turned like oil in the end, our principal dish was good curry, from Singapore we brought with us two large jars of curry powder, and one square tin of red paste this was made of fish and for all the world looked like dynamite in appearance the same grain and all, the nearest is anchovy paste, but this was not anchovy, and in fact since I have tried to obtain it from Singapore but could only get other paste but not the real one, to make curry I used one spoon of one jar powder and one spoon of the other jar, anything in the shape of meat eggs fish could be used, with a teaspoonful of the fish powder I could make a tasty curry, this red paste was the secret of the whole flavour, and many time I have tried since to get it, unfortunately I did not know the name, what a boon it would have been for me in the later days, of course it was not too sweet to smell but it kept wonderfully well, I am speaking about this paste so much because as I had to cook, I can say that I could make a good tasty curry with an old pair of boots if you could chew it, it was like stock in a good managed kitchen. Well now enough with this curry, we also brought a lot of cocosnuts from Singapore which we placed in nursery shape for what reason I do not know, as there was no room anywhere to plant them, not only that but it was prohibited to eat them, when I think of it what a foolish prohibition, when there would never be any reason to plant them. Our biscuits were round and about six inches diameter, and hard as wood it was impossible to chew them unless they were soaked in coffee or soup or any liquid, those were french biscuits used in the navy but when soaked they were very nice, it is surprising what we had to put up with, if we wanted to fry anything it was to be done with olive oil, I remember a dish which I used very often to make, I boiled rice together with salt pork and used to put the young top of the pumpkin leaves and that dish was very acceptable, there was the wild pigeons but we had to go a bit far to get them though they were plentyful our luck was they were not where we were, but sometime Henry used to go hunting at Lambom an Island near by, why we did not get pigeons was simply because there was no fruit trees and there was no food to attract them.

With our poultry we were not too badly off and I must say that our ducks and fowls did very well, but we never killed a fowl.

They were for breeding and only eggs were allowed to eat and we were well supplied with them, the ducks and fowls lay very well, so we were not short of eggs, but I must say that after the other way of living even in our trading station I consider that we were very badly off though not starving, we were only a bit better off than those western story fellow who lived mostly on bacon coffee and beans and some kind of made biscuits out of flour, as I was very young and I had a good appetite anything would do me but those more aged felt it more. One of our great support was the harricots beans in bulk which I forgot to mention, those were very hard as they were dried beans, but with a little care I managed to get them very tender and tasty. As the trip to collect provision was left to me, I rather liked it I would call my friend Massun a native who took to me at first an old man of about forty I should say or fifty, and he and I we would go to Port Breton in the canoe, both of us using the paddle and with fine weather we were at Port Breton in about two hours sometime early if we had the current with us, the worst part of the trip was to pass the point it was very short only a few yards but it was like going through boiling water, with a launch or a boat it would have been a simple matter but with my dugout canoe it was not a joke, however we managed.

At Port Breton I generally took my time, as a rule I went to Mrs. Chambaud who was living the nearest to my approach to Port Breton, and as I liked Mrs. Chambaud very much for her pluck and I as a boy of 14 did all I could for her in my power,[26]

---

[26] This may be one of the reasons why Chambaud himself emerges from Mouton's reminiscences as a pleasant enough character, when the opposite

so first stop Mrs. Chambaud, more likely stayed for lunch, then to the headquarters to get my provision, have a look at the differents peoples and have a good look at Mrs. Dessus who was the wife of an Officer, I generally got my lunch there if I did not get it at Mrs. Chambaud, I remember one day we had some very nice chicken at least it looked like and tasted like, only after meal it turned out to be a large carpet snake, at any rate I must say that it was very nice and tender, I am sure that it was not the first snake Mrs. Dessus has cooked, I was very fond of Mrs. Dessus she was a fine lady very capable and resourceful.

I generally stayed at Port Breton until 4 p.m. then we made track again for our residence, and it was generally sunset when we arrived, as it was the only break we had I took advantage of it.

The people at Port Breton were kiling time by doing useless hard work and this kept going until the malaria fever started, and the provision started to get short and that was not very long after our arrival. We at Bay Marie did the same thing cuting timber and making platforms for our plants and clearing the little land available for planting a little vegetable when we got seed to come.

After about I should say three months by the decision of the Council it was judged necessary that the 'Nouvelle Bretagne' leave for Manila to get a load of provision and also some of the Colons who were supposed to be at Manila waiting, the 'Nouvelle Bretagne' left Port Breton at once and made for Manila,[27] so

---

was more the case (see Introduction). His interest in colonial ventures may have been due to the fact that he found it difficult to find work as a notary in France —at one stage he had to give up a practice in the Dordogne after he had kidnapped (or ravished—'enlevé') the wife of a friend (Lucas-Dubreton 1929: 94). He was sentenced to two years' imprisonment for his role in the Port-Breton affair.

[27] With the example of the two previous Governors in mind, the settlers naturally feared that Captain Henry might not return, and some proposed that his wife should remain behind as a 'hostage'. They eventually accepted his word of honour as a sailor that he would be back in three months. Strictly speaking, the decision was not made by the 'Council' but by the Colonial Assembly (Assemblée Coloniale) which made all major decisions affecting the colony, at least in theory. Captain Henry left earlier than suggested by Mouton—on 16 September 1881. For elucidation of the reference to settlers who were supposed to have been waiting at Manila, see fn. 53.

there was only the 'Génil' left and the 'Marquis de Rays' the Barque we came with, the latter useless as transport purpose but divested of all her sails she was used as an Hospital ship, and it was the intention for which she was bought.

This was rather a long wait and provisions were geting short, so one day the 'Génil' with a few passengers of which I was one of them we went to the coast of New Ireland as far as Likiliki only a few miles from Port Breton, we anchored first at Likiliki where some of the first expedition landed, we stayed there one night then we proceeded up to Mimias we bought taros yams and all sundry food also pigs, we didnt stay long there, the coast was rather open and in case of bad weather it was rather risky.

Mimias looked like a Paradise compared with Port Breton, and those on board asked why not put the colonie there, the land at that place liiked very attractive in appearance, it was covered with alang alang (blady grass)[28] and rising gradually to the hill in a gentle grade, this was dotted with acacia trees, in appearance it looked like a great paddock planted with apple trees, like in Normandie and one of the Passengers who had a right to many thousand hectares Pitoy by name cried when he saw it, and asked why not let him have his share at Mimias, the poor man did not know, that the land was not much good and the hard work it would entail him to make something out of it, Captain Rabardy told him but it was with a broken heart that he left the place, which we did after a night at anchore which was quite sufficient, at that place it appear the morals are very lacking and the crew as well as the natives from Lambom made good use of this lacking morals with the women, the next day we used to barter article of trade such as ax butcher knives beads for provision then we lifted anchore and were back at Port Breton in no time, with a very heavy heart. This few provision could not last long and was only a fleabite for the lot.

From our place at Bay Marie it was very often that we saw aligators passing across the bay nearly every morning we saw them they looked like logs, one day we noticed that one of our ducks was in trouble, an aligator was after him in the water in front of our house we could see the aligator making a lot of fuss, then we saw that he was after a duck, it was very curious to watch the

---

[28] Better known today under its Pidgin name (of Tolai origin), *kunai*.

action of the duck, when the aligator turned to get hold of the duck the latter dived and came up at the aligator tail, it kept going for a while when we thought that the duck may become tired and succumb in the end so we settled the matter by sending a few bullets at the aligator whether we hit it or not we do not know, as he dived and disappeared, a 44 winchester is not much use on aligator, unless the hit is in a very vulnerable spot, though we saw them crossing every day we never shot one, and we never had any oportunity to see one sunning himself, the fact was we did not trouble about them at all, we never saw one coming on our shore and we never lost a duck, the instance mentioned above was the only one we noticed of having been troubled by aligator they must have been very timid, no doubt if we had been careless to go for a swim in the sea instead of the river there would be trouble, about 50 yards from our hut there was a river but not very deep only we had a hole where we could dip and we used it for our bath, the rest of the river was very shallow and of stony bottom we could cross it by jumping from stone to stone, this river was not suitable for crocodile as it was too shallow, and the only fish to be seen was shrimps, the water was runing too fast for anything else, so we were free of the visit of the aligator in the river, however we took good care that there was none about before taking our dip, I think that this hole which was about ten feet long and eight feet wide must have been made by our predecessors which could have been easily done by removing the stones provided they were loose stones really I do not think that any one of us ever troubled how it happened to be there where it was needed, I dont know, I presume we were not observative enough.

The same river one night played us a trick, at about 10 p.m. one night we found ourselve with water up to our knees in our hut rising out of bed we found water and splash into water, our floor being the earth and the hut not very solid we did not know if the whole thing would not be driven into the sea, it was raining heavily and very dark all we could do was to wait, the flood did not seem to rise, at daybreak we found ourselve surrounded by water, fortunately not deep, but all the cocosnuts were floating toward the sea and we lost a great number, with the exception of those we rescued, fortunately our poultry did not suffer they were housed in a bamboo house made for them, and that saved them from being washed to sea, had the water rised higher we

57

would have lost everything, and no doubt ourselves may have been washed into the sea and eaten by aligators or sharks, unless we managed to run up higher land which there was not very far only a few yards.

Another time we had another experience which we never will forget, one day my father Dupré[29] and myself we decided that we would go to Likiliki which was not very far by land, so we took a guide from Likiliki and went on the road so far appeared to be the following of a water course, but when we got over the cape and came to a small bay we found ourselves blocked by a cliff and unless we got a canoe it was a matter for swim we did not think it advisable to risk it so it was agreed that our guide who could climb like a monkey would go to Likiliki and bring a canoe and bring us over, of course to the native way of calculating it was not far, however after we thought that we waited rather long time we decided to go back the way we came, and we arrived opposite Lambom Island just as it was getting dark, now to go along the coast was impossible owing to very tick jungle and also there was several little sandy beach where we had noticed aligator spreading themselve in the sun, the Island is in Straight Praslin and only about half a mile from where we were so we managed to make signs with flare of fire and after waiting a considerable time the Lambom natives came with a canoe, and we manage to get home nearly at day break very tired and with no more envie to go to Likiliki any more, I think that our guide had enough after a long walk and did not feel inclined to come back and so left us to manage the best we could, and we never found out the real truth about the matter.

I think that I now know better that it was rather foolish for us to do because we may have run into a trap and be killed, and perhaps had we waited it may have happen, that was one of the reason why we did not wait we were obliged to reflect a great deal on our escapade, and we thanked our star when we got back, we also were told later that where we passed it was the hunting ground of the kulolon bush native opossum hunter,[30]

[29] A Norman from St Malo, not much older than Mouton. He was the unofficial undertaker at Port-Breton (he made about thirty-five coffins) and became a Hernsheim trader at Vunakambambi near Vlavolo. He returned to France in 1892.

[30] See fn. 41.

who made a trade with the opossum teeth, those were rather wild tribes and canibal above all, as far as canibal goes the Lambom natives were also canibals.

The kulolon natives make practice to go hunting at certain time of the year when there is not raining too much which would be in the south east monsoon, they are about thirty or forty in number they carry their cooked taros they are armed with heavy stick of about six feet long and about one and half inch thick made of hard wood and some possess spears but not many, when they are on those trip their principal hunting is opossum, on each opossum there is only four teeth I think or two I am not sure those teeth are very greatly valued by the natives of New Britain and New Ireland and are interchanged with to nearby natives, in time they are bleached white and are used as collars, the New Britain natives are using them for collar of about 2 inch wide and wear around the neck like the old time collars, the flesh of the opossum are good to eat and the natives are fond of it, they are also hunting wild pig etc.

While we were waiting for the return of the 'Nouvelle Bretagne' a few got the fever, one of the first who got it was Mrs. Chambaud, it was a very sad case, the Doctor had no quinin and this maladie was new to him, however after a hard struggle she managed to get over it after Mrs. Chambaud were a few more Pitoy and his wife died of it, a strong fellow who I saw felling trees only wearing his trousers head and back naked strong as a bull, pay for his carelessness he got the malaria fever and die in a few days sickness and a few more passed away that way.

At last one fine morning the 'Nouvelle Bretagne' arrived after a very long wait, and brought a little hope to the poor peoples it was about time they were very disheartened, but unfortunately when the report of Captain Henry was related we found out that our trouble was not ended. The object of Captain Henry was to buy supply of provision for the people at Port Breton who were on the point of starving, therefore he bought all his requirement, and would be ready to sail again as soon as possible, he was only waiting for the bill to be paid, this however did not come and the vessel was kept as security until payment was made so an embargo was put on the vessel, in such case a part of the engine is taken out so that the vessel cannot leave its anchore without it, what part it is I do not know, but fact is that the ship was kept prisoner and two officers were on guard on boat as well. During that period a typhoone was expected and for the safety of the vessel she was rendered able to go to sea by returning and fitting those part, and during the typhoone Captain Henry let go his cable and sailed away with the two officers on board, and arrived at Port Breton, I understand that he put the officers on a Island not far from Manila, who turned out not worse for their experience.[31]

Two days after the arrival of the 'Nouvelle Bretagne' a Spanish Man-of-war arrived,[32] she nearly got on the reef when she came in and Captain Henry seeing that she was in danger went to her in a rowing boat, after the Man-of-War was securely at anchore Captain Henry was made prisoner, having become liable against the law by runaway with the goods and having contravened against an official while on duty, well that was a bad position to be in for Captain Henry no doubt, but there it was and he had to go through it.

The Man-of-War stayed three days I think to fix matters, it was arranged by the Commander of the Spanish Man-of-War that provision for those who wished to stay would be left, and those who wished to leave could go on board the 'Nouvelle Bretagne' to Manila with the Man-of-war who put Spanish crew on board and kept company until she got to Manila, I father and Dupré and several others remained but the bulk of the expedition went away, amongst them was Schurman, Chambaud, the Judge and a number of the others,[33] also owing to sickness the colons were

[31] They were landed near the village of Dao on Panay Island. Captain Henry apparently expected that about £8000 would be waiting for him in Manila; instead, the Marquis had sent only £1000.

[32] This was the *Legaspi*, a military transport ship, and it arrived on 12 January 1882; another man-of-war, the *Siren*, remained at Zamboanga (on the island of Mindanao), ready to come to *Legaspi*'s assistance should it be needed. 'The Spaniards believed ... that the city of Port-Breton really existed; that, as asserted by the Marquis, it had troops and artillery; they did not know that the title of "Colonel", bestowed by Charles I on his Governors, was in fact an empty gesture' (Baudouin 1885: 204).

[33] The *Legaspi* left on 20 January 1882 with sixty-five colonists and all the indentured Singapore labourers. Forty settlers decided to remain, *including* Chambaud. Of the sixty-five, three died in Manila soon after arrival, a few decided to settle there and the rest eventually returned to Europe. Captain Henry was arrested but was set free in May, after three successive trials by the military, naval and civil authorities. The contents of the *Nouvelle Bretagne* were

very downspirited, and there was a fact, there could be nothing possible at Port Breton, to this day the place is unhabited by the natives, which prove bad enough.

Previous to this happening during the absence of Captain Henry while he went to Manila for provision, there was trouble amongst the governing bodies, when Captain Henry left the Colonie he appointed Chambaud as chief in command,[34] but it was not very long when Captain Rabardy tried to ride the high horse and wanted to be the master, and I think that there may be some fighting if the 'Nouvelle Bretagne' did not return, however Captain Rabardy was not liked, but he was master of the 'Génil' and in the eyes of the poor destitutes the ship was a great asset, as it was the only means of leaving the God forsaken place, so he had a good chance to succeed if Captain Henry did not return in time.

The 'Génil' with Captain Rabardy in command remained with us, in all I presume that we were no more than 30 or 40 the 'Génil' appeared to make some trips of her own sometime she would be away for 3 or 4 weeks, we never knew her movement, the Captain would find some excuse of some sort to make it appear that it was for the good of the people he was doing those trips, even on one trip he went to Bougainville and brought a young girl with him, he stated that he rescued her from the natives[35] he also stated that he was dealing with the chiefs about making everything ready when the other expedition would

---

sold by public auction and included such exotic wares as a number of punch and judy shows, several cases of satin slippers and twenty-two cases of official stationery with the Marquis' coat of arms. The ship itself was eventually bought by the American shipping firm Peel-Hubel.

[34] Before he left for Manila Captain Henry appointed Rabardy as 'provisional' Governor, in disregard of the Marquis' instruction that 'at no price do I want to lose the services of Mr. Chambaud'. However, soon after the departure of the *Nouvelle Bretagne*, Rabardy and Chambaud became 'inseparable' and ran the colony as a 'duumvirat' (Baudouin 1885: 133-34). Since Rabardy was away a great deal during this period (see next paragraph), it is easy to see why Mouton thought that Chambaud was Governor.

[35] Her name was Tani and Rabardy had apparently bought her for two hatchets from a 'King' Kopara. She became attached to her new master and guarded his cabin 'like a dog'. She was almost certainly the only inhabitant of Port-Breton to be upset by Rabardy's death (see fn. 43).

come,[36] one thing is certain, that in some way or other he must have had some influence with those natives because I later on found out that it was mostly impossible to recruit female native on Bougainville, he also had on board a sailor who had been kept prisoner by the Bougainville natives this sailor it seems was a survivor of one of the other expedition who got away with a boat from the rest, he had five or six men with him when he left but he was the only one left, I think that hunger or wreckage was the cause of the other missing, I do not know the name of the man but I saw him on board the 'Génil' very often, I do not think that he was a Frenchman because he had an accent what became of his companions he did not know, but it is more probable that they were eaten by the canibals and part of Bougainville are canibals while the other is not, this I found out in later years, some story go that this sailor was bought by Rabardy from the natives, and that others were kept and killed as they were wanted for feast, but I have no means to ascertain the fact, at any rate it was one of Rabardy's yarns.[37]

I think we must have been about three or four months waiting for news after the departure of the 'Nouvelle Bretagne' but none came we expected one of the vessels of the expedition to come either the 'India' or the 'Chandernagor' and when we found out that it was useless some of the member of the expedition amongst them Dessus and Dupré they took a boat and went to Mioko and

[36] This is presumably a reference to Rabardy's 'purchase' of the entire southern part of New Ireland for a pound of tobacco, twenty-five pipes and some hand-kerchiefs. Port-Breton was to be only a minor depot and the main settlement was to be established further north, on the south-western shore of New Ireland (Baudouin 1885: 110). The man who 'sold' the land to Rabardy, the Lambom headman 'King' Maragano (or Maranganu), was apparently something of a ladies' man and had been chased away from his mainland village for adultery.

[37] The story has been repeated in Baudouin 1885: 113-16; Stephan 1905: 328 and Romilly 1887: 14-15, and probably has some factual basis. The man was an Italian called Boero and he was the only survivor of a group of six who 'escaped' from Liki-Liki in a stolen canoe some time between the departure of the *Chandernagor* and the arrival of the Methodist missionaries. Their destination was Port Hunter but the wind drove them to Bougainville. Five of them were said to have been eaten by the locals; Boero survived because of the ease with which he could burst into tears—'a phenomenon unknown to the natives'. He became a prized spectacle and was safe as long as he could produce tears on demand. He was said to have been bought by Rabardy for two hatchets.

I think Matupi, or they went with the 'Génil' which is more likely, to see Farrell and Hernsheim Farrell was manager at Mioko for a Firm at Samoa, and Hernsheim represented by Schulle[38] at Matupi, it was then agreed to leave Port Breton on the 'Génil'.

This decision was partly due to the fact that Farrell send a cutter a few days before and made approach toward helping for the leaving of Port Breton.[39]

The question became apparent that it was a matter of procuring coal. Hernsheim had no coal but Farrell had coal, as it was a matter of force majeure, the arrangement was then made with Farrell who supplied enough coal to reach Sydney, under the condition that Farrell would become possessed of the ship 'Marquis de Rays' with all her cargo as guarantee for the sum due for coal, if the account was not settled within three months I think.

We were instructed to pack our belonging which was a rather big business for us as we had poultry, timber, and a lot of gears, all the clothing which never been used and I am told enough to last us three years, but nothing was left everything movable was taken away, Farrell had a cutter with a whiteman and a crew of natives, the bulk was moved away on board the 'Marquis de Rays' and the 'Génil' as much as possible the buildings were demolished and the timber carried on board, and all the other goods, when everything was ready we were to move from Bay Marie the next morning, my father went to Port Breton to see to

[38] Friedrich Schulle, one of Hernsheim's ablest traders. He was Hernsheim's representative in Northern New Ireland in 1879-80 and founded a dozen trading stations from his headquarters at Nusa. His successor seems to have lacked Schulle's skill: by 1883 only two posts were left and the main station had been burned down. Schulle returned to Nusa in 1884 and subsequently acquired considerable land holdings in his own name.

[39] Possibly because he was at Bay Marie, away from the main settlement, Mouton appears to have been unaware of the events which preceded the final evacuation. After the departure of the *Legaspi*, a conflict developed between Rabardy and Chambaud (now officially Governor) on the one side and the rest of the 'Forty' led by Dr Baudouin, who were in favour of evacuation. On 4 February 1882 a meeting of the Colonial Assembly deposed Chambaud, declared a republic and decided on immediate departure, by a 'unanimity minus one vote'—that of Chambaud; Rabardy, it seems, either abstained or voted for evacuation. By the time the decision was implemented, on 13 February, four of the 'Forty' were dead.

the arrangement and I was left behind with the remaining gears, that was alright so long there was no unwelcome visitors, I had five or six natives from Lambom[40] with me to keep me company until I was fetched by the boat to take me with the cargo.

To my horror at about 3 p.m. the Gololon[41] hunting party came down they were about 30 men old and young, all armed with the usual stick and other were armed with spears and clubs, this state of affair did not appear to me too healthy, I was sure that loot would be the result so I had all our rifles and shotgun, I gave the Lambom boys the firearms and I kept a revolver and a winchester, toward evening before it was too dark I agree with the Lambom natives that we must do something to protect ourselve against loot and perhaps murder, so I used the building of the place who was strongly build and this was the fowlhouse, this was of about twenty feet long by about fourteen feet wide build of strong bamboo imported from Singapore, as it was build of bamboo against bamboo I could see between each stanchion of the wall, though this would not have been any protection against bullets it was a protection against spears, my only fear was that I may not be able to stop the loot.

Before dark I draw a line on the ground, which separated the natives from the cargo and anything subjected to loot and by means of one of my Lambom interpreters I told them, that if any of them jumped over the line I would shoot him dead and that next morning the other whitemen from Port Breton would be here to look for the cargo.

[40] Comment on the margin: 'Wallis Island native name Laboum' (i.e. Lambom). It was named Wallis Island in 1767 by Carteret in honour of the leader of the Wallis-Carteret expedition and the discoverer of Tahiti, Samuel Wallis. Bougainville, one year later, named it Île aux Marteaux, after the rare 'hammer mussel' (*malleus*) which he found there.

[41] Elsewhere Mouton uses the name Kulolon but in the French version (p. 20) he refers to them as the Golon: 'Golon is a tribe which lives in the mountains about 60 km from where we are'. Baudouin (1885: 277), in a section devoted to the discussion of local customs, speaks of the 'Kings' of Lamassa, Mimiass, Golonne, Candasse and Nomo. Hahl (1907: 310) lists the following 'known' localities on the south-east coast of New Ireland: Mimias, Morkon, Siara, Golon and Lambon (in that order). The Golon, we may safely assume, belonged to the now virtually extinct *men-bush* (Baudouin 1885: 272-73) known as the Laget (which means bush), a 'wild lot particularly addicted to killing native police' (Cappell 1967: 499). In 1905 the Germans taught them the 'customary lesson' and resettled most of them on the coast, south of Muliama.

For all that night I did not sleep a wink and the boys did the same, it appear that it was their interest to save their lifes as well as they were not too friendly with those bush men, only once a disturbance occured, one of the crowd no doubt wanting to test my instruction passed over the line then I fired a shot near enough to make him feel the dirt lifted by the bullet, I see him yet jump in the air I had to laugh, to see his surprise I think that he really thought that he was hit, and I can see the fellows feeling him over to see if he was hurt.

That did the trick and a few minutes after one could hear a fly, they did not go very far, but instead of camping on the premises they camped on the bank of the river.

At day break they showed themselves, but as soon as they saw the boats coming they disappeared like lightning, with the exception of a few cocosnuts they didnt take anything, only they gave me a bad anxious time while it lasted.

Loading our gears took some time then we left Bay Marie for good, our gears were put on board the 'Marquis de Rays' and when all were ready the 'Génil' towed the 'Marquis de Rays' to Mioko this did not take long we started in the morning and were at Mioko before dark.

No sooner we were anchored that a gang of Farrell boys rushed on board climbing from all direction, Dr Baudouin was the only one who stood on the gangway with a revolver in hand, but he was only one against 20 or 30 natives and Farrell, they other people did not even understood what was wrong, from that moment there was Farrell's guard on board, to see that no cargo moved aboard the 'Génil' Farrell had managed to have all he wanted on board the barque, so that he could keep control over it, this was a breach of the contract instead of waiting the lapse of time three or four months he took possession by force,[42] we

---

[42] The contract (also known as the 'Treaty of Mioko') was actually signed about three weeks after the settlers had landed at Mioko, i.e. well after Farrell had laid hands on the *Marquis de Rays* and its contents. The terms were as follows: Farrell advanced the settlers the sum of £900 for a period of four months, and in return the settlers assigned to him the *Marquis de Rays*, including 'all cargo in its holds' (Baudouin 1885: 297). Note also Mouton's earlier comments that Farrell had used similar strong-arm tactics during the loading of the settlers' possessions in Port-Breton; 'I have seen at her house [i.e. Queen Emma's] furniture and valuable objects which came from the colony, and she

could have made him suffer for it if we only knew what could have been done, we had enough amunition and firearms to take Farrell and his staff, but again it was better as it was we may have become outlaws.

After a couple of days at anchore we heard that Captain Rabardy was sick, and went on shore he was sick in the morning and died after a few hours on shore, the doctor did not think that he was that bad and could not understand this sudden death, to his opinion Rabardy was not sick at all when he went on shore only a little indisposition, so the news of his death came to him as a shock, and mentioned the fact, and requested a post mortem to be done but Farrell would not hear of it, and a few hours after death the body was buried, with no proof to satisfy the Doctor, Farrell said that in this hot country the body must be buried at once, so Farrell had his own way, I even was told later that the grave was dug before Rabardy was dead, but it cannot be true, stil that what the rumours circulated at the time.[43]

After the death of Captain Rabardy, there were two things needed now, a new Captain and coal, Farrell had both of them and he did not take him long to settle matters, his interest was to see the 'Génil' out of the way as soon as possible, coal and Captain on board the 'Génil' left Mioko on a fine morning,[44] with all the

---

does not attempt to hide them.' They included the colony's altar (used as a buffet) and numerous family souvenirs, piously preserved from generation to generation—tapestry, embroidered foot-stools, bodkins, grandfather clocks, drawing room tables in Louis XV style, pearl-shell sewing boxes, wedding presents made of precious wood, etc. (Festetics de Tolna 1904: 61-63, describing a 1895-96 visit).

[43] Comment on the margin: 'Doctor [said?] Farrell poisoned Rabardy—his grave was dug before he was dead'. Rabardy was suffering from fever and Baudouin advised him to stay on board for medical reasons; when the doctor last saw him, he was depressed, had broken down and 'cried convulsively'. The rumour that Farrell had poisoned Rabardy was based on the fact that a cup, 'empty and wiped dry', was found near the body (Baudouin 1885: 288)—in other words, Rabardy may well have committed suicide.

[44] On 20 March 1882. The Génil struck a reef off the north coast of Queensland but managed to reach Cairns. After a stop of one month in Maryborough, it finally arrived in Sydney on 2 June, was put up for auction and sold for £2000. Most of the immigrants remained in Australia (five had earlier chosen to settle in Cairns), since the French consul would not repatriate them. Dr Baudouin practised for just under a year in Queensland and returned to France in June 1883.

members of the expedition with the exception of Father, myself and Dupré, Dupré having made the trip before to Matupi had made arrangement to remain and trade for Hernsheim & Co. so no sooner the 'Génil' left Schulle came and took him to Matupi, there was only me and father left at Mioko, at the merci of Farrell.

When Schulle came for Dupré father had a conversation with him and it was agree that we would also work for Schulle, but unfortunately while this was discussed at night on deck of the 'Marquis de Rays' it appear that one of Farrell men understood french Schulle spoke french well so the conversation was carried in french, no one knew that this man understood french, Dupré had nothing to keep back only his own few belonging, we on the other hand had a lot of gears to take in consideration, we had our poultry, utensils, and farmers tools, and all the clothing enough to last us for years, so in a way if Farrell wished and wanted my father for his own purpose we were not free to dispose of ourselve as we liked, it must be understand that Farrell took advantage of our ignorance regarding the possibilities, we were absolutely ignorant of the natives ways and the little we knew was to make us believe that we were practically in the hand of Farrell, we stayed at Mioko for at least a week, during that time there were discussion between father and Farrell, he wanted father to work for him and even at that time he had the ambition of starting a plantation in New Britain, and wanted father to be his manager, of course there was an excuse for Farrell, he thought that father being associated with Schurman was the man he required believing father experienced planter he probably in his imagination was quite honest, but on father refusing the job on the ground that he was not competent to take the job on, which was the fact but Farrell being an Irishman did not believe it, so this was the cause of further trouble with Farrell later.

Farrell did all what he could to torment father so that he made a contract with him as trading on one of his station, not having succeeded with the plantation business, father was rather reluctant to settle any agreement because he thought that news of the expedition may come yet before it was too late,[45] and at last

---

[45] The expedition Mouton refers to is almost certainly that which left Barcelona for Manila on 1 September 1881 on the *Barcelona*. The contingent consisted of a

Farrell got tired of the whole matter and make use of a very simple ruse, which was if you do not sign this contract you will never see your son again, and it was a fact that though I was not a prisoner I could not come in speaking distance with my father, I must say to the credit of Farrell it was done neatly and no doubt he was very conversant with the ignorance of new chums, of course father could not do anything else than to sign the agreement under protest which did not avail him of any advantage, and there we were engaged by force you might say for Farrell, while we would have preferred to deal with Hernsheim, of course in those day it was our believe but on later experiences one was not better than the other, at that time the usual rule was 100% on goods and six pounds per ton for copra.

When time was ripe for Farrell to make use of us, he send us to New Britain to a place called Ravalien where he had a bamboo hut, the man in charge of the boat which was only an open boat was a russian who spoke french and also a little native, his name was Rosenthal a young fairhaired fellow,[46] he brought us at the place and gave us a few instructions how to handle the business etc. he stayed a couple of days then he left us, with the understanding that we were sufficiently conversant in the way of buying cocosnuts from the natives for trade goods such as beads, hardware, tobacco in stick called twisted tobacco imported from America 26 sticks to the pound, also firearms was sold to the natives.

At first things seemed very strange but we managed to act as we were told and the method was to pay one stick tobacco for a number of cocosnuts ready shelled and ready to cut, for a gun we would receive so many hundred cocosnuts clay pipes also was

---

number of settlers plus a group of Sacred Heart missionaries (see fn. 53); they were to be taken to their final destination by the *Nouvelle Bretagne*. In the French version (p. 25) Mouton says 'father had faith in the Marquis' and that he intended to wait for three months before signing an agreement with Farrell. Dupré apparently felt the same way. He blamed the failure of Port-Breton on the squabbling, laziness and insubordination of the colonists, and is reported to have said: 'If only the Marquis had come with us—how different things would have been!' (Poulain 1883: 153).

[46] Baudouin (1885: 295) refers to him as a 'Russian nihilist who had taken refuge in these distant lattitudes'.

a great trade with them specially those representing a nigger head or something else, the more fancy it was the better, but the most usual clay pipes in those days was the one with a ship in full sail, calico was also an article of trade but not much, the natives were thoroughly naked men and women the only covering they had was on their neck or arms, and only those near the Mission wore loin cloth, in one instance I saw a young girl who had a loin cloth and when she came to sell her goods to me before coming she took off her loin cloth which is called lavalava, she did this quite unconsciously, simply as a matter of habit, Farrell after a little while supplied us with an open boat rigged with a main sail and jib, of about 20 feet long but with a fair beam so as to stand the sail, with this boat we were able to move about and get more cocosnuts, not far from where we were there was a German Trader called Coenen who was about five miles further on the coast called Ralum, this trader was one of the survivors of the 'Chandernagor' who cleared out and left them, those had to make shift and drifted to the mainland of New Britain and Mioko, and were distributed by the firms Hernsheim and Farrell to the different trading station on the coast of New Britain New Ireland and outside Islands, who were doing the same thing we were doing.

The principal article produce we were buying from the natives were, where we were cocosnuts which we dried in the sun, this took three days to mature if there was fine sunny weather, and more if rainy weather, this consisted of the flesh of the cocosnut cut in slices and spread on mats made of cocosnut palm leafs, which the natives made and bought at twelve for a stick of tobacco,[47] we used to spread them and if fine weather left them until dried but when the rain came we had to bring them in heaps and cover it with other mats to protect it from the rain in such

[47] Although Mouton had missed the golden days of the copra trade (1878-79) when a stick of tobacco could be exchanged for up to forty nuts, when 'axes, knives and firearms would fetch as many nuts as were asked for' (Parkinson 1887: 85) and when copra sold in London for between £16 and £22 a ton (Blum 1900: 169; Finsch 1887: 525), his profits were still considerable. A pound of twist tobacco cost about 1/9-2/– f.o.b. in Sydney. With twenty-six sticks to the pound, the 6000-6500 nuts required to produce one ton of copra would have cost him no more than £2. Most traders prepared the copra themselves; if local labour was required, it could usually be procured for one stick of tobacco a day.

case it was a matter of quick work, to get the boys to do the work, when the weather was favorable there was no trouble and some-time it took only two days to dry, and made a very good white copra.

From the beginning father never recognized the agreement made with Farrell as valid, to him it was a forced one, he had to sign on the point of a revolver, we threatened by a man who was not better than a pirate, he wanted traders he forced them, he threatened us to be left amongst the natives and do the best we could, we did not know the natives then so it was a very serious threat in our eyes, he even one day told father that he would take me away from him.

On that ground father did not stay on Farrell's property, and after a couple week we started to buy a piece of land at Kokopo and build a house better than the hut we were in, and when it was completed we shifted in to it.

Farrell at the time did not make objection of our shifting as long we were dealing for him, and we were quite at peace for a while with Farrell, unfortunately the natives were not civilized and we had to be very careful how we dealed with them, they came to the market which was a fixed day every three days, that day the natives would come in great number and barter with copra or cocosnuts for trade, between the market day very little business was done, they would sell a few cocosnuts only, the proper business day was the market day.

It was my business to take the boat and go to Kinigunan[48] to buy cocosnuts, and even as far as Kabakaul, I would return with a boatful this helped to produce more copra, in those day the natives were armed with spears and tomahawk, this consisted of a fantail hatchet with a long handle of about three feet long the end of it was ornamental with some carving figure and painted with red, white, yellow, this handle was made of hard wood and polished, the spears were made of palm wood and about nine to ten feet long, pointed at one end and at the other generally bone or feathers the latter was very pretty, it was an art to make them,

---

[48] Today's Vunanami, referred to as Kinigunan in most early records. Powell (1884: 79) uses Kininigunun and Parkinson (1887: 78), Kininigunan. Note that it is an area not a village; thus 'Kinigunan is that area that I will call Vunanami' (Salisbury 1970: 21).

they were made of different birds feathers green red white etc, the bone consisted of a human thigh or a cassowary thigh bone, the human thigh bone was very much appreciated owing to the fact that it represented the fall of an enemie, and when I asked them about it they would mention the name and state that he killed him in a fight, and he was quite proud about it too, others were armed with club, they also used a sling made of pandanus leafs and the string made of fibre twisted like a rope, with this they throw hard round pebbles of about the size of large plum, some of them were very accurate with it. I saw a native kill a bird from a tree, and many clever feats done with it, those pebbles are very hard and like blue metal, one of their clubs is made of a round stone the size of an orange, in the middle is an hole large enough to take an ordinary stick of about one and a half inch diameter of hard wood, the stick is fixed into the hole the top of the stick is thicker at the head so as to keep the stone secure and finally it is kept solid with putty made of native plant one of them is a fruit like a chestnut the kernel of which is scraped and when this is dry it become very hard, in fact the smell is very much like linseed oil, with this putty they manage to make a very good solid job and the stone remain firm, the stone is generally found in river bed, the stick is about four feet long, it must be the work of patience to drill the hole, and it is made stone against stone, a small stone is secured by putty and string to an handle and this is manipulated by a bow, it is of very slow progress but they have plenty patience, and this implement is very efficient I can assure you, the handle being a little flexible give it powerful impetus.

We were also armed and it was not out of place in the point of view of the natives, the beginning was very trying owing to the attitude of the natives, at night one of us was keeping guard while the other slept we were specially doubtful about our firearms, and we were new in the country having no knowledge of the natives custom, and while doing our dayly duty we had a revolver in holster ready for any emergency, I found out later that it was not quite necessary, but who know. On one of my excursions for copra at Kinigunan, I had an accident, the sea was very choppy and the boat rocked very badly, I gave instruction to my crew who had muzzle loaded gun to load the gun but keep the cap out of the gun and there would be plenty of time to put the cap, well this instruction was not carried out, so when the boat started to rock and the natives showing rather nasty on the beach, my crew feared an attack and got hold of the gun, one of the guns fell against the rib of the boat and the gun went off, a bullet entered the abdomen of one crew and one nipped the tip of the ear of another.

There I was in a very bad fix, the natives on the beach started to yell and my crew started to pull for all they worth to get out of the place it was fortunate for me that they were not on good term with the beach natives, the natives followed the boat on the beach up to our place when I arrived it was low tide and as soon as we touched bottom the crew left me the sand from the boat to our house was about fifty yard and I had to pass through two rows of natives all armed ready to drop me, I with my carabine in one hand and my revolver in the other I kept going, to this day I cannot understand why I was not killed, because it only required a knock on the head and it would be the end of course I would have killed one of them before one could kill me but that was all the next one could kill me easy, I managed to reach the house father did not know what had happen until I reached him then the natives were into the house looking for our firearms fortunately they were behind a box out of sight, with the exception of the revolver on father there was two winchesters and shot guns, my father got hold of an axe and making moulinet[49] with it got the natives out of the house.

We shut the house and we were surprised to find one of our boy with us, the natives outside send stone after stone against the house and tried to get hold of any vulnerable spot, we fire above their heads we did not want to kill, it would be the last thing we would do, however while there was a lull I got out of the house to see what was going on, for my inquisitiveness I met a native with spear poised over me and in avoiding the spear at the same time I fired but missed the next movement he was at me with his tomahawk to finish me but I had time to reload and he was too late, and he realized it as well he jumped clear out of my sight behind banana plants, I had the spear in my thigh, father pulled it out when I reached the house, I bandaged it with an handkerchief and looked for targets but could find none, I do not know what happened but the natives became more cautious and it was under shelter that they kept slinging their stone, it was good-bye to our fowls and anything portable outside, however

[49] A gallicism; *faire moulinet* means to flourish.

we manage to get the boy who was with us to send word to Coenen who was only no more than five miles from us, he came with his boys and that was the end of the trouble for that day, when the attackers saw Coenen coming with his boys they cleared out for their lives, the spear got about six inches in my thigh as the attacker was above me he throwed his spear in a down way direction and only got the flesh downward, the main thing was to keep the wound clean, which we did with carbolic water as soon as we were under calmer condition, it is the custom with the natives that we were responsible for the accident and with the help of Coenen we paid the relatives that settled the matter,[50] and when we did our part we got the natives to return some of our poultry, and in a few days we got them all nearly back.

The next day in the morning half dozen natives came down, and passed rather uncomplimentary remarks about our marksmanship, so to prove that they were wrong I made a circle on a coconut tree near by about the place where the head stand, then I went about fifty yards and shot two shots in the circle, then turning the gun in their direction I told them if they did not clear out quick they would have it, of course it was a point necessary to re-establish our prestige, and even I would have shot to kill in that case, fortunately it was not needed.

The native who speared me had to pay ten fathom tambu[51] to me to settle the wound he inflicted on me, it took some time but at that time I was more conversant in native customs and gradually the matter was settled, and thereafter our intercourse with the natives got on better to a certain point.

It was after that that father made arrangent with Coenen to get his supply from him, this was rather foolish because Coenen was dealing with Farrell, in fact it was more than foolish because though we did not deal direct with Farrell he did not loose anything, we were dealing for him indirectly, only it made Farrell rather wild about it. Later we had reason to feel Farrell's revenge, Coenen for his part did not threat us too well, then father found out his mistake, we did not bring matter to better understanding, I think Farrell having gone so far thought that father was playing

---

[50] According to the French version (p. 31), the man who had been shot in the stomach died—a fact which is not mentioned here.

[51] Shell money; Mouton refers to it in several subsequent passages and also in fn. 82.

the game, and the attitude of our trying to avoid Farrell made him anger toward father, then Farrell claimed the land we bought from the natives as his property, on the ground that we had no right to buy the land for ourself, father defied him, but it did not do any good, at last father made arrangement with Hernsheim and then we shifted to Kinigunan where father made another house, but before father did that, father refused to give the boat up to Farrell on the ground that we were in credit to about double the value of the boat, of course now I can see that father was wrong, well it happened that father pay a visit to Father Navarre at Nodup that is I think in 1883 or 1884 during the night the boat disappeared Farrell who had his people watching took advantage and took the boat, father returned home with a native canoe, and we had no more boat, so father made an agreement with Hernsheim & Co. and we shifted to another place Kinigunan as mentioned, father tryed to claim the land at Kokopo but Hernsheim who was German consul[52] advised to let it go, it is very unfortunate we did, but at the time Hernsheim aim was to get father free of Farrell.

I may mention that Father Navarre with some other priests came by the 'Chandernagor', who landed them[53] and went away again, only stayed a couple of day, she went to some place and was confiscated for debt.

[52] Appointed by the Imperial Chancellor under the provisions of the law of 10 July 1879 concerning consular jurisdiction. His powers as regards German subjects were broadly similar to those exercised over British subjects by Romilly as Deputy High Commissioner for the Western Pacific.

[53] As mentioned in fn. 45, several Sacred Heart missionaries sailed from Barcelona on 1 September 1881 to re-established the Vicariat of Melanesia and Micronesia, vacant since the evacuation of the Woodlark Island mission in 1855. The group consisted of Father Joseph Durin, the mission Superior, Father André-Louis Navarre, Father Théophile Cramaille, Brother George Durin, a nephew of Joseph, and Brother (later Father) Mesmin Fromm. According to Dupeyrat (1935: 42), the move was initiated in 1880 by a group of Sacred Heart missionaries who had settled in Barcelona after being exiled by the Ferry Government, and in March 1881 the order was formally requested by the Sacred Congregation for the Propagation of Faith to supply missionaries for the venture. The group arrived in Manila about the same time as Captain Henry, left for Batavia on 9 December 1881, spent five months there waiting for further instructions and finally reached Matupit on 28 September 1882, after a journey which took them to Singapore, Cooktown and Sydney. From Matupit they went to Nodup where they stayed until April 1883 when they moved to Kinigunan.

By that time after having our boat taken we did not take long to move to Kinigunan, father having already arranged to make a hut this is made with bamboo and in a few days it is done.

We are now under Hernsheim & Co. contract, and so far we are clear of Farrell, Hernsheim supplied us a boat the usual thing in those days and we are keeping trading in the usual manner,[54] Farrell never gave us our extra clothings and the timber he kept that, I presume he thought that he was entitled to it, some of those goods were from Hauterman family and had nothing to do with the expedition, but that did not stand good with Farrell later on it was a common thing to see some of Mioko natives wearing our cloths, however I think now had father been a little more diplomatic and kept trading for Farrell we would have been much better off, by changing we did not better ourselve and made an enemy of Farrell in the bargain, all my father's complaints to the German Man-of-war or to Hernsheim were of no avail, they only laughed at my father. The German officers when going to Mioko were invited by Farrell who explained matter in a different way, together with champagne dinner to wash it, there was no chance in either way to have justice.

With the 'Chandernagor' came the Sacred Heart Mission, Father Navarre, Father Cramaille and Brother Vatan[55] who landed at Nodup where Father Lanuzel one of the first Missionars of the Sacred Heart Mission who came with the Marquis de Rays former expedition who landed at Nodup had a hut build there. Father Lanuzel came by the 'India' I think that he went away by the 'Génil' to Sydney when she left.

Nodup was not very large piece of land and after a little while Father Navarre bought a piece of land at Kokopo from the natives, and shifted to Kokopo, the hut they build was made of grass just a roof over the ground that is a two long bamboos as frame spaced two feet apart and bound together by strip of bamboos like lattices fastened with ratan (or kanda) on this grass was attached up to the pointed head, it must have been about

[54] The boat usually became the trader's property after he had delivered so much copra. In the case of Farrell's traders the quantity was set at twenty tons, or £120 worth of copra (Baudouin 1885: 289). Hernsheim's terms were presumably the same.

[55] Not Brother but Father (Louis) Vatan. He did not come with Navarre on the *Chandernagor* but with Father Fernand Hartzer and Father Benjamin Gaillard in March 1884, almost two years later.

forty feet long or perhaps fifty, this was only a makeshift, and I think that they had trouble at Nodup with the weather, one day in a heavy storm they were nearly washed out of Nodup, Nodup is at the foot of the Mother and where they were situated was just on the side of the mountain so a heavy storm brought torrent of water rushing down and taking everything with it fortunately they were installed on a little knoble and that saved them, but it was enough to warn the priests that Nodup land where they were was not a place suitable for the Mission, it was impossible to make any progress there.

Here again Farrell showed himself, not against us this time but against the Mission, he informed Father Navarre that the land was his property that he had bought it from the natives some time ago, on information it was proved to be false, and Father Navarre was quite satisfied that he was in his right and Farrell in the wrong.

About a month after the mission was installed at Kokopo and thinking of making arrangement to get material from Sydney, and quite contented that they had a start, a catastrophe occured during a dark night the place was on fire, from our place father and I we heard the explosion of bamboos, and sure enough we saw the Mission on fire, we rush to the place which was only about fifteen minutes walk and there we found the Missionars moving all they could from the fire, they saved very little but fortunately for them the fire started at one end and saved the main important matter such as documents etc. by the statement of the natives which I managed to investigate, the cause of the fire was one of Farrell's doing, he did not want anybody installed on the land and he made provision that it could not be done, however in those days there was no mean to get justice, and this matter had to remain as it was for the present.[56]

The fathers stayed with us for a while then they bought a piece of land at Malaguna in Blanche Bay and shifted there when their house was build of native material, but this time they were wise

[56] It would seem that Mouton was right in his belief that Farrell was to blame for the fire. See, for instance, Hueskes (1932: 27): 'On the instigation of a white settler the straw hut was set on fire during the night of 27 June 1883,' and Jouët (1887: 66): 'It was not the Kanakas we suspected, but a Whiteman . . . a Catholic . . . may the Lord forgive him!' Salisbury (1970: 27) says that the mission records in Hiltrup 'make veiled suggestions that this was done at the instigation of Methodist teachers at Vunanami'.

and made their house with proper walls and roof forming a shed, with partitions as required, it was the best move they could do it was no use for the Mission to fight Farrell, for one thing they could not prove that Farrell pay a native a gun to do it, fancy a grass hut reaching to the ground on each side what a fuel for fire, the native set fire by throwing a charcoal which caught fire by the wind, at night there is a land breeze blowing as a rule, the native knew that and for two reasons the native used this method, first it was quite simple to carry a bit of charcoal which would not be noticed, while a fire torche would be seen, on the second consideration the escape would occur before the fire started, very clever for an alibi, but in this case it was not the aim, the aim was to get away out of the way undetected, of course I found out all this much later after having kept inquiries it must have been some months before I got the truth, but what was the use as Father Navarre said there was only prove for them that it was done intentionally, but very dangerous to act on those indications, and beside there was no court, and that settled it, the best conviction on earth would have been of no use.

The Missionars were very well supplied with provisions and all church ornament in silver and other metal, they had divided the hut in two portions, one part they lived in and the other they used as store as the fire started from the living part they saved a little but all the church ornament we found them melted, it was by accident that the fire was detected in time to save their life, I think Father Cramaille was the first to notice it and gave the alarm, at that moment it was just starting, so they moved what they had time to move before the big blaze started, which lasted only a few minutes, when Father Cramaille notice the fire his first move was to get the chest which contained the documents, amongst them was the title made by Father Navarre with the natives confirming the purchase of the land, in those days it was the only way, make an agreement like stating the lay of the land to the best of knowledge as stated by the native proprietor who showed the boundary, and signed by the native by a cross and witnessed by some whiteman,[57] the witness was my father such

---

[57] An example of an early 'properly executed conveyance' (between Farrell and a group of Duke of York villagers) can be found in Sack (1971: 176). The document specified the sum the villagers received for their land (£52 in goods), described in extremely vague terms the land in question ('one thousand

document constituted a legal title of purchase, and no doubt if lost would be rather hard to duplicate, the original native perhaps been informed to keep off the transaction in future by party concerned.

While this occured our friend Dupré was established at Vuna-kamkambi on the north coast of New Britain for Hernshein & Co. and was doing well he was out of all the troubles, and it didnt take him long to master the native language, and so did I father could only manage the pigin English so far only a word here and there, it was when the Mission had been some time at Malaguna that Father Navarre started to buy land at Vlavolo with the help of Dupré it was an easy matter, Vlavolo was only about six mile from Vunakamkambi on the coast, the usual communication was by boat or canoe, or by native path along the coast.

While Father Cramaille was stil with us I had another narrow escape, father went to Mioko in our boat and was rather late in coming back and the natives began to show nasty, to their mind father and the crew met with an accident and perished, though we did not think that it was the case, I heard the natives discussing the share of our body as a feast, one say he will have an arm the other part of the leg, etc. it was very unpleasant to hear my own body and Father Cramaille's to be divided by those hungry wolfs by the way of their talk, at the time I was quite conversant enough with the language to understand what they were saying, but the natives did not know yet, they thought that they could boast for all their worth at my expense, owing to bad weather father was three days in coming back so Father Cra-maille and myself had a very unpleasant waiting, father at Mioko could not very well with the bad weather, we knew that it was more likely the case but it did not suit the natives way of thinking, in their heart they wished that father and crew perished, so that they could kill us and take possession of our belonging, and by the way they were talking have a good feast out of us, it was only the second day that the natives showed restive and the third it

---

five hundred acres more or less') and concluded: 'We the undersigned acknowledge receipt of payment in full. We further declare that we are the right and lawful owners of the above described land, in witness thereof we have subscribed our names.'

was practically settled that it was a fact, then I told father Cramaille that the natives said and that we must prepare for the worst.

I had plenty guns for trading at the time because we used then for sale to the natives, so beside my winchester and revolver, we loaded all the guns I had ready to be used, and we could shoot through the wall between bamboos, so the only thing to do was to wait events, I did not think that they would do anything at night but will start in the morning that was the fourth day, as we did not know at the time exactly the custom of the natives we were on the qui vive[58] all night but we were prepared to sell our life dearly.

At day break father returned with the crew and all well, I then noticed that some of the natives were rather disappointed, and showed long faces, that settled all their boasting, I did not forget to make use of their boasting, to shame them, they were quite surprised when I told them what they were saying, owing to the fact that I was responsible for the crew according to their custom I should have been their victim or pay the pot.

Amongst their unjust rules some one has to pay for the lost one, whether it is your fault or not, in this case they would put the blame on me and Father Cramaille, and for this reason they were all painted and armed to the teeth, no wonder that they were disappointed when father turned up, having gone all that trouble for nothing, they did not reckon on our defence at all, now that I know the natives it is a toss up if we would not get the best of them, because I found out that in all their fighting very seldom there is many victims, and as we were determined and we would have shot a few before they could get us.

Our present dwelling was rather too near the creek and while there was a storm we were nearly washed away, so we decided to shift, this time we made a rather fine house, on piles and the walls made of small bamboos or rather a kind of cane the thickness of the little finger, this worked in two layers made a good wall, for floor we had made of palm strips nailed on bush timber frames, compared with the other dwellings that was a palace, for the first time we did not have the soil for floor.

---

[58] On the alert (literally, 'who goes there?').

It was year 1885[59] that we noticed that Farrell was buying land from the natives, also noticed that others were doing the same so we follow suit, with my knowledge by that time of the natives language and very well acquainted with their custom it was very little trouble for me to purchase land, at that time I was no longer with father while father was at Kinigunan I was at Kabakaul about four mile further east, I thought if we did not buy land we would be left in the lurch, the only trouble was to have Hernsheim & Co. to make an alteration on our contract, by allowing us to buy land for ourself. Fortunately for us Hernsheim was not inclined to buy land at that time, had we been with Farrell we never have been able to buy land he wanted all for himself, in no time with my knowledge I managed to buy the land, something like five thousand acres in all, I would have bought more which I had ready fixed with the natives at Kabakaul but father did not want it, it would be a matter of a couple days and a little trade which we had, father missed it and Farrell bought it, this was a great mistake from my father because it proved later a good asset for Farrell, it would have been very important for us in our trading business, poor father could not see further than his nose, we had the means and he did not take it,[60] and what a boom it would have been it was more mortifying to me because I kept the natives from selling to Farrell I had all the names done and it was only a matter of paying and make an agreement, I have been very sorry that I did not take it on myself, but I think at the time I was not quite 21 years old, it must have been something like that which prevented me, because

[59] Either a typing mistake or a mistake of fact, since the land rush was virtually over by 1885. The date should be either 1882 or 1883, more likely the latter, if only because in the next paragraph Mouton says: 'It was just at that time [i.e. early 1883] that Farrell started the Ralum plantation . . .' Fn. 60 is also relevant here.

[60] Mouton Senior came to regret (though apparently only half-heartedly) his lack of business acumen. 'I have bought much land, I don't know how much because I haven't been able to have it surveyed. It cost me 500 dollars, three or four years ago. I could have bought the whole island for that sum' (Mouton Senior to Madame Sapart, 18 March 1886). In the same letter he said: 'We are happy and contented, better off than the likes of us in Belgium.' Note also his comment that 'life is more relaxed here than in Europe' (Mouton Senior to Monsieur Armand, 2 July 1885). Both letters are in the possession of Mrs Sturrock.

I have regretted that my father never took the opportunity to take advantage of my having all fixed for him.

It was just at that time that Farrell started the Ralum plantation Farrell brought from Buka 150 labourers and started to clear the land at Ralum where Coenen was about one mile from his station, one named Parkinson[61] whom he brought from Samoa started for him, this has proved very successfull enterprise.

While this was in progress we were still trading for Hernsheim, then for the first time we got opposition, next door to us about half a mile from us, Mioko Agency put a trader named Brandt, the latter was one of the survivor of the 'Chandernagor' expedition, a German by nationality.

Brandt having been in business on different part of the Islands for Mioko Agency, was very much more experienced in the way of trading, and he would have been a very strong opposition for us, he also had instruction to buy land from the natives, fortunately for us he did not receive what he wanted to do the business and came too late, I understood that he was a little disgusted with his firm, he was not too anxious to see the firm having the land so he did not trouble about buying what was left, and there was plenty left, for a while, he could have had a good slice, but when he got the goods to buy Farrell was ahead, Parkinson made a big sweep for several days he was busy buying for Farrell.

Brandt proved to be a good neighbor, and we divided the trading business pretty well, but unfortunately he did not stay very long the firm send him on other station, and put another one with instruction to make a strong opposition to us, for a time it was copra war, the rule when he came was twelve nuts for a stick of tobacco and we were not doing too bad, the next neighbor started to put it down at ten nuts we did the same, and he put it

---

[61] The son of an Englishman who had settled in Schleswig-Holstein, Richard Parkinson was born in 1844, taught English in Heligoland, went to Samoa in 1877 to work as surveyor for Godeffroy and Son, married one of Emma's sisters in 1879 and moved to New Britain three years later. He worked for the New Guinea Company between 1889 and 1900 when he rejoined Emma's business empire. He was an ethnologist of repute and published some twenty articles and two monographs, including the monumental *Dreissig Jahre in der Suedsee* (1907) which had been translated and edited by N. C. Barry and is available in typescript form in several Australian research libraries. He died in an accident in 1907. For a sympathetic portrait of his wife Phoebe see Mead (1960). She died in New Ireland in 1944.

down even less so we fixed this matter on a different principle when it come to six cocosnuts for a stick of tobacco, after the mark ten for a stick we put it for less two nuts at the time but we only used a few pounds of tobacco and would not buy more and so on we let him have it, and brought it down until by continuing buying as he did he was buying at a loss he made the copra all right, but when it came to reckoning he was very much in debt to the firm, the firm only paid for a ton of copra six pounds and in Mexican dollars[62] at that per ton of 2240 lbs. so it did not take long to make a mess of it, then the Mioko Agency came to the conclusion to give it up, and it was the last of the opposition.

In 1884 the same year, the Germans hoisted the German flag in front of our house and we heard on all the different Islands so the Island became German colonie, previous to that the Germans had started trading. Farrell himself though he was of Irish descent managed for Godeffroy established at Samoa, the Man-of-war who hoisted the flag in November that year was 'Elizabeth', then for the first time we had officialdom to deal with, the first Official was Van Oertzen[63] established at Matupi and acting as German representative under the title of Commissar.

In 1885 Von Oertzen gave instruction that all the selfmade

[62] Latter-day relations of the Spanish dollar current in New South Wales around 1820, Mexican dollars made their way into South-East Asia after 1850. Although the New Guinea Company had introduced German Imperial currency into the Protectorate in 1887, cash transactions continued to be effected largely in pounds sterling or in Mexican dollars. Because of the presence of coolies from Singapore and the Dutch East Indies, they were particularly popular in Kaiser Wilhelmsland, even though their value was subject to considerable fluctuation (between 2/3d. and 3/–). In 1899 the Mexican dollar was worth only 2/1d. on the Singapore money market (Tappenbeck 1900: 535).

[63] Arrived in New Guinea in June 1884 to represent German interests under the direction of the German Consul-General in Apia, and became Imperial *Komissar* or Commissioner after annexation in November 1884. A *Komissar*, in the German colonial set-up, was a Governor in all but name 'sent out in the early stages, when German policy was based on the idea of protectorates to temporarily look after the affairs of a colony' (Leutwein n.d.: 15). As *Komissar*, Von Ortzen prohibited the recruiting of labour for non-German territories, the selling of arms and ammunition to villagers and the buying of native land without official permission. Although the New Guinea Company was granted an Imperial charter in May 1885, the first *Landeshauptmann* (Administrator), Vice-Admiral von Schleinitz, did not arrive in Finschhafen, the first 'capital' of the colony, until June 1886.

titles should be presented to the Commissar with an approximated measurement given for acknowledgement, we did what was wanted. Dupré did the same, to our surprise Dupré had no difficulty and Von Oertzen acknowledged his title Dupré having also bought land on the north coast where he was, those agreements had to be translated in German, the Mission in that case helped us, some of the Fathers were German and they obliged us with fixing the translation.

The Mission themselve could not understand why Von Oertzen refused to acknowledge our titles which were in order according to instruction. The reason given by Von Oertzen was that the land had been bought by Farrell and that he claimed it, all father's explanation was of no avail. Von Oertzen would not recognize father's claim.

This was very clear to father that Farrell again was behind the scene and with his Samoan girls and champagne he bribed the poor fool Von Oertzen,[64] there was no use to claim any more all what father did was to write the truth to Von Oertzen and the same to Hernsheim, of course from Hernsheim he got the cold shoulder and disapproval for using such terms and reasons, Von Oertzen was quite wild with father, even it went so far as to cause trouble in our trading.

Farrell again had the help of a German Man-of-War to act for him, we had established some huts on the coast with natives as traders on the land we bought, Von Oertzen gave order to the Man-of-War to destroy all the huts which they did, so we were again against it, the reason for Farrell's action was to prevent us to take possession in any form of our property.

Father wrote a very long letter to the Belgian Consul in Sydney explaining the situation as it was, father addressed the letter to

---

[64] Farrell's *modus operandi* had been commented upon by several contemporaries. 'We were enjoying our cigarettes and beer, when one of the Houris of Paradise arrived on the scene . . . Her appearance completely took our breath away . . . She was of medium height . . . with the bust of a Venus, and with supple limbs like alabaster . . . Was it to be wondered at that my friend was enchanted by the vision, when two such hard-hearted mortals as K-h and I were sensibly affected?' (Pitcairn 1891: 167-68). See also E. Hernsheim, 'Memoirs', p. 152, quoted in Sack (1971: 185): 'The nice and approachable nieces and cousins did not fail to make Ralum the centre of attraction of all unmarried employees of the Neu Guinea Kompagnie. Queen Emma herself, like the Empress Elizabeth of Russia, could accomplish miracles in love making and drinking.'

the Belgian Consul Sydney Australia, knowing that it was of no use to use the usual post which was only by any vessel chartered by Hernsheim or Farrell, and that it never would be posted, father acted differently, he gave a sovereign to a sailor and told him to post the letter at the first port the ship made the ship was a three masted barque loading copra for Hernsheim, and brought coal for Hernsheim who was the provider for the German Navy. The sailor kept his word, father having explained that it was important and that the ordinary way would not be safe, after a lapse of time of nearly a year, father received a message from Van Oertzen to send all his land titles to him for registration, a few days after we received a letter from the Belgian Consul from Sydney, stating that the matter had been forwarded to the foreign Minister in Berlin and that he is instructed to take notice of our claim, the same as the others, the reason why father did not get the letter sooner is because Von Oertzen was not too sure of himself and asked father to leave matters as they were and not to mention anything of what had happen, father told him that the only blame he could find in him is that he was a weak man, that Farrell was the culprit.

It is quite clear that if father had not used this stratagem to circumvent Farrell, any ordinary way to send a letter to the Consul and even to other address would never have reached their destination, for the simple reason that Von Oertzen knew that he was doing wrong, and Hernsheim would take the part of Von Oertzen, and as there was a kind of a mailbag made for any ship available for postage for the public and the Government, any letter from father would certainly have been censored.

I think that it must have been in the year 1886, that Hernsheim made a proposition to father and Dupré, to enter into partnership and conduct Kinigunan and North coast together, he proposed to supply goods at so much above cost prices and buy copra at so much a ton. I forget the term of the transaction,[65]

[65] The contract, which ran for two years, was signed on 1 November 1885 between Mouton, Dupré and Co. (the partnership was formed at the same time) and Hernsheim. The terms, as they affected the Moutons, were as follows: Hernsheim supplied them with a cottage and a boat each and agreed to supply them trade goods at 20 per cent above cost price ('more than 50% cheaper than before'), while he continued to buy their copra at £6 per ton. In November 1885 the Moutons had only two trading posts; five months later they had five (Mouton Senior to Mme Sapart, 18 March 1886).

Hersheim then supplied us with a weatherboard cottage, but he would not build on our land so we sold him the land where the cottage was to be erected, the cottage came from Sydney ready made all we had to do was to erect it, that did not take us long to do, at the same time I was supplied with cottage also but only made of pine wood and build by a chinaman carpenter, but it was a great improvement on what I had, I took great pride in it though it was very simply build, two rooms and a five feet verandah, the whole thing in these day would not cost more than £25 the plank were not smooth I could only use white washing on it, the plank were 12 × 1 in. the frame was made of 2 × 3 hard wood, so now we are in partnership Mouton Dupré & Co.

This partnership turned out to be a failure, while father and I were economical Dupré was extravagant, having goods seemingly cheap he got himself and in no time we were in debt, the partnership did not last very long father saw that if we kept going as it was we would be more and more in debt, and worst than ever so we disolved partnership, Dupré went to Vunakamkambi on the north coast, he bought the land himself and could deal with whom he liked, however he had to deal with Hernsheim so as to clear part of the debt, and I believe never changed.

In the year 1887 we had a very severe plague of dysentery the natives died like flys,[66] at the end their tomtom did not sound any more, every day there was a funeral, our house was like an hospital. I did what I could for the natives, as well as our people, so far we were escaping the epidemy, and then father got it and it has been a very hard task for me to look after him, even he was so bad that I had to require the asistance of the Doctor of the German Man-of-war 'Marie' who was at Matupi, the Doctor came at night he gave me strong laudanum to give father, after a while I got him nearly right when he made the mistake of eating some water melon, that foolishness settled it, he got a relapse from which he never recovered and after an illness of seven months, he went to Cooktown with the 'Ysabel' and died at Cooktown Hospital a fortnight after arrival.

A very strange coincidence happened, Father Navarre then at Cooktown was present when father died, at that time Father

---

[66] It is indicative of the value of some of the New Guinea Company official publications that its annual report for 1887 or 1888 does not mention this fact.

Navarre was no longer Father Navarre but Bishop Navarre,[67] he performed the last religious ceremony for father it was in the year 1888 that occured, father must have had a presentiment when he left because he said, my son I do not think that I will ever see you again.

Now at the age of 22 I was left by myself, at the time there was no cultivation, our house was surrounded by the jungle we just cleared enough land to dry the copra and room for the different sheds, our mode of transport was by boat or canoes, the access to the native villages were by native narrow winding paths, that narrow that one had to walk one after the other, at either side there was thick bush or kunai grass about three feet high, and sometime another kind of wild cane of about seven feet high, the village as a rule was situated on a cocosnut palm patch, just enough clearing for the village their backdoor was the jungle the village were not very large, a large village would consist of about twenty huts, and the next village would be about ten minutes walk this of course in New Britain at Kinigunan where I was stationed, the natives had their little garden or rather taro patches which they shift every year, the planting or crop was taro, yam, sugar cane, banana, sweet potatoes, and sundry crop used as cabbage, when a crop is finished and the last is banana they let the shrub take charge of the patch, and go further, the same patch may be used again in three years time, this is to give the land rest instead of manuring I understand.

All I had at the time was a little trade goods the land which we bought from the natives, the money necessary for father's passage and expenses I owed to Hernsheim & Co. and the epidemy which kept everything back fortunately I escaped the epidemy, and with the exception of Malaria fever I kept pretty well in good health, though there was a time when father was alive that I was so bad that father gave me up, but I got over

[67] Bishop since November 1887, Archbishop after August 1888. He left New Britain in August 1884 and spent a part of the next three years on Thursday Island and later on Yule Island off the Papuan coast. He became Apostolic Vicar of Melanesia in May 1887 and, after the establishment of a separate Vicariate of New Britain in 1889, remained in charge of the newly created Vicariate of British New Guinea. He was Superior of the Yule Island Mission until 1907 and died in Townsville in 1912.

it, father also has had his share of malaria then, and very bad too once I thought he would die from malaria.

In the year 1888 the New Guinea Company had started in New Guinea and had a station on the Duke of York group, on the Island of Kerawara[68] and the place was too small for the Government also was too far away, and it was suggested that they would shift to New Britain.

While father was there he would never let me go recruiting, so when my chance came I went to New Ireland with my open boat to recruit this time I was fortunate enough to get fine weather, and after been away a week I returned with six boys from Kokola, this was my first start in recruiting, it was not much but it was a great help for me, at New Ireland I found a German who was trading at Katolik [Kadelek] I stayed the night then the next I left for Kokola, this German by what I could see did not do any good there was not enough copra for him to make a living and could not understand a Firm making such mistake, later I understood that the plan was not so much the copra but a footing for recruiting labourers for the plantations at Samoa,[69] stil even in that line the man was the wrong man for that job, and I think that he got very sick or he was killed by the natives I believe through his fault, I understand that he lost his head and provocated his end, myself I found him very funny the way he lived, he had a native woman with him and I think that is all he thought about.

With my six boys I was more independent of the local natives, and I was able to work better and made more copra, but at the time my contract with Hernsheim was nearly expired and in preparation of such emergency I had a bamboo hut build on my land at Tamaluban in case I should not agree with Hernsheim

[68] The date should be 1886 rather than 1888, and the place Matupit (also, New Guinea should read Bismarck Archipelago). The station was transferred to Kerawara in 1887 and functioned almost entirely as an administrative post and recruiting depot until it was transferred to Kokopo in 1890, on the suggestion of Richard Parkinson. The company eventually developed extensive coconut plantations in the locality.

[69] Mouton is referring to the D.H.P.G. According to Schnee (1904: 370), the firm sent about 250 New Guineans to Samoa in 1903. Ten years later there were still 786 New Guineans on the island, not counting a hundred women and twenty children.

& Co. this place was only about five hundred yards from where I was.

The schooner 'Soe' came and took my copra that finished my last transaction of my contract with Hernsheim, then he made me a proposition to sell the house land [and] boat for £210, two hundred and ten pounds which I accepted, under a contract made by Hernsheim my debt to him on this transaction was seventy pounds, under the term that if I did not pay it within twelve months the property returned to Hernsheim, and the money paid by me one hundred and forty pounds forfeited, this was nothing so far I was sure of myself, but what made the transaction unjust is that Hernsheim would only accept copra for the value of goods they supplied that is that if I bought for twenty pounds goods they would only take copra for the same value, and when I asked Hernsheim how he expected me to pay the seventy pounds I owed if he did not buy my copra, he told me that it was my business, and I showed him that it would be, and a week after that interview, I was clear of Hernsheim, in the following manner I went to Mioko the next day and borrowed the seventy pounds from the Firm Deutsche Handels und Plantagengesell-schaft, and made a contract with them so as to dispose of my product, Hernsheim did not like the idea to see me settle so early, but was quite willing to take the money and give me a receipt for it, but I did not see the business done that way, so I went to Kerawara and made inquiry to the administrator who was also a judge,[70] and owing to the term of the contract of very vague tenure Hernsheim had to pick me up with his launch and only I paid him the seventy pounds in the presence of witness.

When I come to think of it, what was the business idea Hernsheim had in his head not to allow me any means to pay him off, did he think that I was too simpleton to find my way clear, if he did he got a shock. Hernsheim was a jew[71] and no doubt thought he would get the best out of the bargain but to my mind a very stupid way of doing business.

Mioko was now occupied by the Mioko Agency and Farrell

[70] G. Schmiele, resident judge in the Bismarck Archipelago from 1886 until 1891, Administrator of the Protectorate between 1892 and 1895. He died in Batavia in March 1895 on his way to Germany.

[71] Comment on the margin: 'Hernsheim dark with moustache'.

was now on New Britain at Ralum where he had started business for himself, on the same line as he had managed before.

I was fortunate at the time that a German recruiter who had made a good recruiting trip could lend me the money for six per cent, Fring the manager for the Firm could not do it it was against his power, but he managed to get Kline the recruiter to let me have it, I never paid any interest in a month the money was paid,[72] I was rich in native money and I used it to buy copra, so as to be clear of that debt as well.

This native money of that part of New Britain is a cowry shell of about quarter inch long and white, this shell is pierced at the back so as to be stringed on a part of the inside part of ratan used like a string and the way of value is per fathom from arm to arm, for small dealing it is by hand length, or finger length, at the time I could get four bags of green copra for one fathom, but it gradually got less when my oponent started the same game but I did not care much I made use of my chance.

Following that year at the end of 1889-90 the New Guinea Company offered to buy some of my land at twenty marks per hectar, but to be able to sell, it was necessary to have the land surveyed, so they send a surveyor Mr. Bernard Linnemann, he came to my place with six New Guinea boys I offered my help but he did not think that he would need it, the first day he made a track from the beach near my house in a south direction this was only to have a good knowledge of the lay of the land.

In doing so he came to the first village and his line came through a village and straight on to a house, of course the natives in those days were not civilized yet knew me but objected to be disturbed, and did not understand that the house would not be touched, but nevertheless the surveyor had to leave his work and come back, the natives having threatened to kill him, so I offered my service in future, I left a boy in charge of my business which was very easy to manage, all I had to do was to give him enough trade to carry on which I checked on my return from the day's work with the surveyor, this lasted twelve months this gave me a good experience regarding surveying land, and also my trading

---

[72] In the French version (pp. 60-61), Mouton says: 'I went to Mioko . . . and Mr. Fring lent me the sum at 6% and gave me goods, etc., but I only received £6 per ton for my copra. I paid it off in three months.'

was not complicated and it was very important for me to know the lay of the land as well, the first village we came to the line cut right in the middle of a native hut, at first the natives thought that we would destroy the hut, but when I explained that the hut would remain as it was and when they saw the deviation we made they understood and there was no more trouble and the surveying business went smoothly as long that I was present, we started at six a.m. and returned at six p.m. it was rather hard work but I was young and I liked it, at one period we had a German with us named Lausen he did not like the work it was too strenuous for him and after a few days he gave it up he could not stand it, and we were very glad when he left he was so clumsy that he was never out of trouble.

After the land was surveyed the part bought by the New Guinea Company amounted to 445 hectares which I sold to the Company, I received the payment in New Guinea gold pieces,[73] unfortunately I used this money as current money instead of keeping it as a curios, but it was also required for my need, and I could not do two things paying my debts and keeping the gold.

Mr. Linnemann could speak french so we talked french, unfortunately for me it would have been better if he did not I would then have learned german instead of him improving his french, after having made some exchanges to equalize my land I think I got about £250 in N.G. gold pieces, and my land of Kinigunan Plantation as it was called amounted to 1100 hectares clear, it was at about the year 1891 that Mr. Linneman became ill and he had to leave as soon as possible he left with the 'Adler' a German Man-of-War, I never heard any more about him and I do not know if he stil living and if he ever reached Germany.

During those years 1890 and 1891 my boys did a bit of clearing but six boys could not do much, so I tought of employing local natives I managed to recruit one hundred of them and the work was going on well at that time my plan was to clear all the cocos-

---

[73] Between 1894 and 1898 the New Guinea Company minted its own gold, silver and bronze coins, similar to German coins in size, form and metallic content. They remained legal tender until April 1911 but had disappeared into collectors' coffers long before then, partly because of their unusual design which featured the bird of paradise. As early as 1897 the twenty mark coin (worth officially one pound sterling) sold in Singapore for 23/–, and for as much as £5–6 in Sydney about a decade later (Leidecker 1916: 49).

nut patches I could get hold of in my property, with those hundred boys I did a good job because the clearing consisted in falling bush and burning when necessary, by doing so I become master of all the old cocosnut trees planted by the natives, the natives at the time neglected those trees and would not look after them they said that they were too old and could not bear more, but a year after my clearing when they saw that the old trees were breaking from the weight of the nuts they saw their mistake, however having gone to the trouble of clearing I took possession of the cocosnuts and it gave me a good help yearly it was a steady income which has helped me to make my plantation it was at that time that an epidemy of influenza raged and after about two years work my local labourers left me, and I found myself only with the six boys I had, fortunately I had not much land planted and those six boys could keep the land under controle for a while, my plan was to fell as much as possible so as to prepare for the future, the big timber being felled I had only the new growing timber to tackle, and I found out that it helped me a lot, instead of planting as I was going along I cleared and let it grow again, by so doing I gained later on having only to clear the small bush.

Many a time I took advantage of a dry spell and bush fire, the fire would clear the undershrub and leave the trunks which were felled before and all I had to do was to clear the rubbish and burn what I could, in such a way I managed to plant in one month what it would have taken six months to do and even more. Of course I had to wait until the land was registered before I tackled the clearing this was the advise of Linnemann when I told him of my intention, the land was registered soon after the sale to the New Guinea Company and I had not to wait very long it was a matter of a few months. I planted my first cocosnut trees in September 1891 on my westerly boundary on the beach, at that period I had only about ten hectares planted.

Now my boys were due to be returned after three years, and it was time that I made preparation to get some more recruits, to replace those six and get more if possible.

In 1892 I borrowed Father Cramaille's boat Father Cramaille at that time was stationed at Vlavolo on the north coast a few mile from Dupré his boat was larger than mine, but also an open boat, so with a crew of six I started for New Ireland we had a very good wind behind us and we reached Kokola in no time, landed the boys with their box,[74] then I started to recruit but I was informed that I would not get boys before the feast was finished, and it was a feast all right there were hundred of natives from different villages, and for a week dancing was in progress, and to make matters worse the weather was very bad there was a strong South easter blowing, I had to get the boat dragged on shore as she could not lay at anchore for the sea was very high and the shelter was no good for South east wind the shelter was only suitable for North west, at the time I did not know that so I was trapped.

The natives promised that when the feast was over I would get boys and we stayed at Kokola for two weeks, during those two weeks while the feast was on, there was dance every day and it would not have been good policy not to be a spectator, it was necessary for our life's sake to show no fear, however I took certain precaution in doing so, with those of the crew who would come with me I arranged so as to be placed in such a way as to have my back protected, at Kokola village the front on the beach had a cliff with a drop of ten feet then under that a sandy patch not more than twenty feet, the situation was very favorable and nothing could come from that side if there was a good stand high up I would take it, without showing it, I would do so under any excuse if I was asked to sit at another place by the chief, for at least eight days it was unbearable and we had to be present whether we liked it or not, after the dance was over I could see that there was no chance to get boys, for one thing the weather was too bad, and I think the natives did not like it.

There was a day when the sea became calm and boys or no boys I decided to shift to another anchorage, this was only a quarter of a mile further and the shelter was behind a reef only big enough for a small boat like mine, at high tide the swell was very bad, we stayed during one night, in the morning I woke up finding my oars gone, at once I knew that there was something doing, the oars could not have dropped by themselves while we were asleep some one must have come from the shore and take then.

I went on shore and when asked the chief for the oars, he did not know and thought that the oars must have fell in the water, then as he was showing rather an insolent attitude I pointed my

[74] See fn. 95.

revolver at him and told him if my oars did not turn up I would kill him, this had its good effect and within five minutes my oars were returned. Previous to shifting when we were at the first place we had some trouble also, at night one day we noticed that the women and children disappeared from the village and toward night not a soul to be seen, I naturally expected trouble, some of my crew started to frighten and wanted to drag the boat into the sea, but this could not be done if they wanted owing to the impossibility of moving it, however I told them to go to the boat if they could shift the boat, amongst my crew there was only two that I could rely upon, so as the other did not know what to do with themselve we three kept watch all night ready to fire at anything showing if an attack was made, at daylight I and Jemy one of the boys, we covered ourselve with branches representing a small brush and walking very slowly we got into the village and we saw no one, then we thought that no doubt it would be for later on, but the indications did not point that way and I could not make out what to make of it. Only later in the day a native got more pluck and came near us and we learned from him the reason of this proceeding.

It appear that a smart fellow spread the rumours that we would take some boys by force and take them away, and the fools believed him, so we were afraid of them and we could not make out what we may expect, both parties were afraid of each other, for our trouble we had a nasty anxious night without sleep, and the native I think did not fare much better, they were not very far away but they did not make use of their huts, so they must have hidden in the bush.

To return to my last anchorage after I got my oars back in such a forceful way I judged that the native were very unfriendly and only watched their chance,[75] so when I saw that the weather was a bit smooth we started and we managed to make Labur a distance of about 30 miles there we found a fine anchorage, sheltered from the South east. I found the natives rather friendly, and we stayed rather a long time waiting for fine weather meanwhile I recruited twelves boys, that is ten boys and two girls, my provision were getting short and my tobacco which I used to buy

[75] About three years later they did take their chance and ate the entire crew of another trading boat. A punitive expedition visited the area in 1896 (Hahl 1907: 311).

provision such as taro and native food was at an end, however I must say that the natives gave me all I wanted.[76]

While I was at Labur I wanted to get cocosnuts to make oil for our guns but could not get them at the village I was told if I would go to the next district with them they would give me plenty cocosnuts, of course I accepted, I was only too anxious to get oil I did not like my means of protection to be neglected, the fire-arms must be kept in order.

Very early one day just as daylight started I and my boats crew with all our firearms followed the natives over mountains, we were kept going for rather a long time, and to my reckoning the palm trees were only a few miles from the beach while we were going over mountains along the coast, I could see that there was something wrong in this expedition, but there was only one thing to do in this case follow and keep quiet, it was no use to make a row we would have no chance with them.

By the sun I judged that it was about noon, and we heard a great comotion from some distance from where we were coming our way I did not know what to make of it, and we were prepared to defend ourselves if needed, then only I was told the reason of the great uproar and sure enough some warriors dressed in their fancy painted attires feather headgear and body painted, were carrying a child victim of about five years old, he was not quite dead he was fastened by the hand and feet with a stick through, the stick was carried on the shoulder of two warriors and the poor victim still crying and bleeding, went along to is destination, I felt inclined to put an end to his suffering by putting a bullet into his head, but I was warned not to do that.

We arrived at the village in triumph like and the victim still alive was put down in a kind of natural depression into the rock about four feet deep, and about twenty feet diameter, round shaped, then the natives thrust taro bananas sugar cane and all the material to be used as food for the feast, the first throw which was taro killed the victim and put him out of his misery, and I was very glad that the poor child did not suffer any longer.

For three days the natives were in glory, there was dances every night and gloryfication, it was fortunate that the weather made it impossible for me to leave or I would have left sick of the

[76] 'I was well received by the Chief Bahar . . . I had run out of trade goods and he gave me provisions on credit' (French version, p. 65).

94

whole business.[77] The morning after this expedition I received another surprise, at about six or seven in the morning there come from the north point of the bay we were in I saw about twenty or thirty natives all painted white from head to foot, brandishing spears and tomahawks dancing and coming toward us, I at once collected my boys and there we were ready for the worst then a native came to me and told me that there would be no harm coming that it was an acknowledgement for the service we did in enabling them to have a revenge against their enemis, in fact as those warriors reached us they said, malumalum malumalum[78] and throw their spears at my feet sticking them in the ground.

Though I had to show that I was not afraid, I was not too sure when I saw those savages all painted white whitewashed with lime it was and they looked rather uncanny.

I was informed later the reason of their deceit, they wanted the protection of our firearms to protect them in their raid they were making on the next district to revenge themselve of a similar raid. One of the enemis had a shneider rifle and they were afraid of him and thought of using us for protection, it was quite correct according to their way of looking at it, the raiders must have gone a lot earlier than we did because we only met them coming back they had killed a man and his wife and brought the child to be eaten, I presume the child was easy to carry, or they did not take the time to carry the three victims, those victims were simply innocently working in their taros patch when they were massacred, it is their way and the enemis had done the same some time ago, with the protection of the chief who had a rifle, so it was eye for eye and blood for blood. After the excitement of the white warriors, everything went very nicely and when the victim was properly cooked the native presented me with a piece of the child, which looked like pork, I told them that whitemen were not eating each other like them, so I refused and for a good while after when they offered me pork cooked in stone like they do, I could not eat it the resemblance was too great I could see in my imagination the child carried and bleeding.

[77] Comment on the margin: 'Was given a piece of the boy but says Octave I never ate it.' In the French version (p. 68) Mouton says he was offered 'a piece of human flesh, on leaves, with taro and bananas'.

[78] 'Translated' in the French version (p. 67) as a 'sort of homage'. In Pidgin, *malumalu* or *malmalum* means soft, tender, soggy, swampy.

I got my cocosnuts all right the same day but not from the effect of the expedition they brought them from a nearby patch, not very far away, I proceeded to have those nuts scraped and the milk squeezed this I boiled in one of my saucepans until the water evaporated and leaving only the oil, which was better than letting my guns rusting.

Not very long after this experience we had a chance to leave so we made a start, we managed to start for an hour or so then my boat shipped too much sea and we had to return but this time we found a little rock Island just enough to shelter our boat, I did not want to go back to the village because where we were ready to make a start at any moment the sea showed a little dullness, seven times I tried and each time I had to come back, boat shipping too much sea, being an open boat there was no chance to keep afloat. After our seventh trial we managed to make a start, the sea having abated a bit I found that the boat could face the sea and we kept going, the current was so strong that instead of reaching my place Kinigunan, we reached Dupré's place at about four o'clock in the afternoon, the first thing I asked is a cup of coffee I had been without coffee for twenty six days, Dupré being a Frenchman knew how to make coffee.

I just arrived in time it was arranged that the 'Ysabel' the steamer of the New Guinea Company would go and look for me, so I did not arrive too soon, I stayed one night with Dupré then left for Father Cramaille changed boats and left for my place, arrived there in the morning having sailed during the night.

My return did not seem to be welcome by the natives, and I could understand why, you should think that it was the opposite that they would be glad, but nothing of the sort.

On asking the explanation, one of the chiefs with whom I was very friendly told me that they were tired of me and that I better look out for my skin etc. so I could see right away what was wrong with them, they did not care for my coming back but wanted my native money a kind of cowry shell strung to ratan, all my poultry were gone curtain on the windows were gone, I noticed that practically all movables were gone, fortunately they respected the room where the native money was stored.

At first I could not understand the reason, which become quite clear to me afterward, a loot would mean that those who get it first would have the lion's share and the others next to nothing.

Well on my arrival those signes were not too confortables, and I was rather uneasy expecting trouble in the morning, in the morning the natives came in an unusual number, they showed provocation and their disappointment, the chiefs came first to interview me while the rest of the crowd kept under cover, so we had an argument and I asked them what was wrong with them, their people were back and what was their reason for looting the place and showing disappointment, receiving very belicose answere, I come to the conclusion that it was no use talking, and the only thing to do was to show fight.

So I gave instruction to my boys to be ready, I placed them in different place so as to be in good position, then I went to the chiefs and gave them a bit of my mind, and told them what their intentions were and the reason of their disappointment, then I took my rifle and fired at a cocosnut palm and told the chief if he did not get out at once the next one would be for him, also that I wanted all my poultry back and each chief has to pay me 10 fathoms diwara, that they were in the wrong and that I required reparation, of course this was a bluff, though I had my boys in very good strategic position, we were 20 to 1 still knowing their method of fighting I had a good chance and they knew it too, they knew if we picked our men there would be no resistance, and to make sure of it I did not forget to tell them what I would do, knowing their leaders I mentioned their names as my target, this had a good effect, because they knew that me being in the know that I was right in presuming what effect it would have on the attackers, so instead of attack they went away with the good knowledge that they would have to return all the stolen poultry and material and pay me the 10 fathoms money I asked.

Their threat to me were that it was a pity that I was not eaten by the new Ireland natives and also that they were tired of me and that they would kill me to get rid of me etc. I let them have their say and then I shouted at them what they were, and my shot to the palm calmed their temper a good bit, as explained above.

For eight days return of stolen things came little by little until there was very little missing, the chiefs pay their fine as I requested, after that I was very popular with them, they knew they were wrong and when we were in peace I explained what would have been the result had they continued in their attitude, and they saw that I was right, first by me shooting the leaders as they showed themselve the rest would clear out, second the white men would punish them for killing me and my boys.

At that time I was very good in the native language I could talk like themselve and knew their rules perhaps better than themselve, this of course was a great advantage, which they did not realise until it had to be put to practice.

It was in 1892 that Dupré took a Holiday to Sydney and to be able to do that he asked me if I would look after his place, it was a hard job, because I was starting plantation and my place was 10 miles by water to Malaguna and from there over the mountain to the north coast on foot another 8 miles or 10 miles I should think, his business was only trading with the natives exchanging cocosnuts for trade tobacco print, calico, axes, spade, gun powder bead etc.

Dupré had about 30 undertraders each received goods on credit, therefore my job was to be at Dupré's station every three days, I would then collect the cocosnuts on the market place check the lot and replace the goods, I generally managed to do it in the morning I would leave my place in the afternoon I had a guide with six rowers sleep at the station and be ready for 8 a.m. if the work was not too much I left the same afternoon or next morning at daybreak, the drying and cutting was controlled by Dupré's boys, I was young and healthy and there was no red tapes to put up with so I had plenty of time to do it nicely. Dupré returned at last he only stayed about a couple of months, he was glad to be back again, and I was more glad than he was because it was an ungrateful job, after his return I could put all my time to my plantation and trading business, while Dupré was away he found out that he was better off than when he left, if he had known he could have stayed in Sydney longer, it was all right for him but not for me. Now the same road I used to walk, one can go with motor car from my place to where Dupré's Station was in a couple of hours, it took me the good part of half a day by boat and by foot.

Dupré was very neglectful in keeping his accounts in fact I was very surprised to see that all the accounts he kept was what the Firm made for him that is the usual statement, with the exception of the native traders he kept no accounts at all so I tried to made up an account book for him, though I did not know much about bookkeeping I had a way of my own which showed how I was standing and what special matter of my business stood, however when I left Dupré reckoned that it was waste of time to keep book, all he wanted was to know to what extent he was in credit with the firm, so it was easy for him he did not want more, what profit he made on copra did not matter to him, all he knew is that if he sold the trade cheaper than a certain price he would be the loser.

Well Dupré having tasted civilization did not remain very long before he had a craving to go home, so before I knew where I was I was informed by Bishop Couppé[79] that Dupré intended to sell his property and go to France, on this information I offered Dupré the same terms as the Mission and that he could return if he wanted, but it was no use he accepted £300 cash and £80 yearly remittance as long as he lived, I must say that Bishop Couppé acted rather unfaire and behind my back before I could reach Dupré again the bargain was done.

The matter would have not interested me a bit, only for the fact that being only two friends we made our will to each other, a few years previously, in this case I found it necessary to have this will cancelled before Dupré leave the country, I had a little trouble about it but, with the help of the German Magistrate at Kerawara Dupré had to inconvenience himself and come with me to Kerawara and destroy the will, Dupré from some reason I cannot account for had objection to have our will cancelled, and pretended to say that he had property in France and would compensate, I said this was made for this country not for France, his relation had more right to what he has there then me who has no interest in France at all.

It is a very strange thing that Dupré and I were very great friends we were like brothers, but after he left he never wrote to me, so end our friendship for ever, the only news I received was from the Mission ocasionally.[80]

---

[79] Ludwig Couppé, the 'real founder' of the New Britain Sacred Heart Mission. Born in France in 1850, he joined the order in 1880, spent a part of 1885-86 as a parish priest in Sydney, went to Yule Island in mid-1886 and was sent to New Britain late in 1888, together with Fathers Hertzer, Thomas and Goutherand. He became Bishop in October 1890 and remained in charge of the New Britain mission until 1923. He was elevated to Archbishop in 1925 and died in Sydney in 1926.

[80] 'After about a year he wanted to return but the mission could not advance him money . . . he lived for another ten years . . . the mission paid him £1,000 in all he could have had £2,000 but he refused he was afraid that if he had all this cash he would spend it foolishly' (French version, p. 72).

Before going further into my experience, I must describe the natives custom,[81] specially in the neighborhood of Rabaul Blanche Bay and principally Kinigunan about ten miles from Rabaul in New Britain, and next to Kokopo, however the custom extend to a great area of New Britain, if not exactly it does not differ to a great extent.

On the child coming to the world, which is about the same as the general rule only the midwife is a native woman who has some experience in the matter, during childbirth the mother is kept in her hut with only the attendant, the rest of the family husband and all have to keep away for the time being.

As soon as it is permitted the midwife make a fire near the hut, and take the child in her arm and balance the child over the smoke and say, for boy; you will be a great warrior like your father, you will be a good cultivator like your father, and even you will be a good thief like your father etc, that is if the father has such reputation, and so on all the virtues or sins of the father are mentioned, if it is a girl it is the same only as the mother.

Up to the age of ten or more a boy has not much to do only amuse himself, perhaps he may help his parents if he feel inclined, his principal pastime is to exercise himself with sling spears etc. the girl is not so fortunate, from childhood she must help her parents with the cooking and gardening, as soon as she can walk she carry a basket on her back and supported from her forehead

[81] No attempt has been made to annotate the ethnological comments which follow. There are several useful accounts of the way of life of the Tolai people around the turn of the century, for instance Parkinson 1907; Kleintitschen 1906; and Hahl 1897. Also useful is Salisbury 1970. Although the French version devotes less space to the description of the local customs, it has a section on cannibalism which does not appear in the English version. The description of the 'manner on preparing the victim' (pp. 48-49) deserves quoting: 'He is suspended by his legs from a tree and they start a fire under him . . . and scorch his hair and skin with twigs of straw after that they cut open his stomach and remove the intestines and then they cut off his head and arms and the pieces are distributed in the various villages. To roast the rest they start a huge fire they dig a big hole in the ground and fill it with stones and when they are red hot they remove the fire and some of the stones they wrap up the meat in leaves put it on the stones and place on it the remaining stones. All this is covered with leaves and soil . . . Sometimes they start a fire on top if the piece is really big it may take a whole day before it is properly roasted.'

by a band of string made of bark, as she grow she become used to it and I have seen women carry three big baskets made of cocosnut palms, filled with green copra weighing 50 pounds each making a load of 150 pounds, and in such a way the women are beasts of burden, they do all the carrying you may meet a gentleman leading two or three of his wifes all loaded to full capacity, while he only carry his weapons consisting of a sling which he carry around his head, and in his hands two or three spears and a tomahawk or a club, the handle of the tomahawk is about four feet long the head is a fantail hatchet and the part used as the hand rest is about eight inches by five carved and ornamented with feather, before they could buy the hatchet they had only clubs made of hard wood, and under his arm the inevitable betel nut and all his little belonging, the gentleman having no pocket as he is only wearing the cloth he was born in, and so are his wifes, not even a loin cloth or leaf, like some other parts of the Island, if the gentleman has the luxury to have a clay pipe he carry it on his armelet made as a rule of plated fibres, of which he carry one on each arms.

The natives of New Britain and even in New Guinea and I know that they have in the Solomons Buka and Bougainville, New Ireland, are divided in two totem which is represented by a bird or fish, to make this totem clear I will use the totem used in New Ireland, as in Kinigunan they have not adopted a name to distinguish the difference but know the difference by using as a root one or the other principal family, therefore by using the New Ireland method I will be able to make matter quite clear, I understand that there is very few whitemen who have a grasp I am sure there were none in 1886 and even in 1895.

Now I will call one totem eagle and the other totem hawk. The children are taking the totem of their mother, if the mother is an eagle the father will be a hawk and so the children will be of the eagle totem, therefore no eagle can marry an eagle he must marry an hawk and vice versa, this has its advantage that it prevent blood mixture to be too close, a cousin from the mother side can not intermarry, so in their way they keep the close relationship quite apart, this also include the method of distinguish the ownership of land property, if the land belong to an hawk descent this land will remain the hawk and so will be the case with the eagle.

This knowledge of the totem distinction become very valuable to me in ascertaining the owner of the land we purchased from the natives and later enabled me to refute any later claims made by the natives, with the knowledge that the land had also the totem of the owner. Say for argument sake, a hawk claim that the land has not been bought by me and that the land is his property, I at once inquire from the natives present if the land is an hawk totem or an eagle totem, I am told that the land is of eagle totem, that settle it the claimant is only an impostor, he being an hawk he could not be owner of land of totem eagle.

An hawk must marry an eagle totem, so the parents select a bride if an hawk into an eagle totem, if the bridegroom is a hawk his bride must be an eagle, the uncle maternal as a rule select the bride for his nephew and having selected the bride call at the bride parents and bargain with the price for the bride, the price is from ten to fifty fathom diwara the price vary according to the influence of the bride's family, the uncle of the bride having accepted the money the bride is kidnapped and brought to the bridegroom family, at the same time the bridegroom is also kidnapped and brought in a secluded part in the jungle where a hut has already been build, he may have to stay hiding for a month, during that time he is not allowed to move from his hiding place, but while there he is well fed and well looked after.

The bride may only be of only ten years of age, and the bridegroom about twelve sometime eighteen rarely older.

On the date arranged the bridegroom is brought to his uncle's village which has been decorated for the ceremonie, but while the bridegroom was still in his hiding place the bridegroom's parents have distributed to the bride's parents and relations all kind of articles, such as food fruit article of trade such as knives, axes beads etc.

The bridegroom is dressed with all fancy painted on his body and wearing a necklace bead or opossum teeth collar etc. and brought to the selected place in the village where a mat also decorated is on the ground, he then kneel on one knee and carry a club on his shoulder, keeping his eyes on the ground, he is not allowed to look at the spectators for fear he may look at the bride's parents, the end of the club rest on the ground and the rest on his shoulder.

Then the bride's relations bring before the bridegroom their tribute, this consist of diwara[82] which they deposit on the mat and represent the value for the article they received from the bridegroom's parents, this vary from half fathom diwara to ten fathom.

The ceremonie terminated the bridegroom's uncle take charge of the tributs then the bride return with her parents and remain with them until such time the bridegroom is able to take her, that is until maturity if she is still too young, the bridegroom is free but his trouble start, it is their rule that the bridegroom has to return to his uncle as much possible the value of the bride, to that aim he has to do something, to pay back the ten or fifty fathoms diwara, which he do by means of fishing if he is on the coast selling the fish or making taros patches, this he sell for diwara according to price ruling, in such method he accumulate the price of his bride, also if he become a dukduk it will help also to collect some diwara toward the repayment, after the first wife has been bought he buy as many wifes as he like, it is only a matter of being able to pay the price, after the first ceremonie there is no more ceremonies, in some instance the bridegroom may be twenty or more and his first wife only ten, then he get a second wife and he is able to bring his first child wife to his second wife and remain with him as his property.

This is rather a grave offence, an eagle commit an offence with an eagle girl, she may be a far-off relation or no relation at all it is sufficient that both are of the same totem, this is called Pulu an unknown witness to the party call in the middle of the night at the uncle's or brother's village of the criminal deposit before the hut's entrance a cross made by two sticks of a plant Tanget a kind of croton with variegated leafes, in the morning the relative see this and know there is trouble ahead, but he do not know yet what to expect, then the next night he hear a voice stating the fact that so and so were guilty of pulu.

When this ascertained the uncle or brother of the culprit hunt for him and bring him to the village, then in the presence of spectators he is decorated with flowers and painted in the same similarity as in the marriage ceremonie, he then is placed befor

[82] Comment on the margin: 'Shell money worth about 4s. a fathom comes from Nakani [i.e. Nakanai] coast'. The term *diwara* was traditionally used on the Duke of York Islands; the New Britain word was *tambu* or *tabu*, depending on the locality.

the executor who is the nearest of the family who club him with a club, a tomahawk is not allowed to be used.

The body is then carried in the bush and buried there in a disgraced manner, the woman which may be a young girl or an old woman is killed and generally eaten, there is no fuss about her she disappear either in the ground or in the belly of the natives.

It is fortunate that it do not occur very often, during the forty eight years I have been there I only know one case, of course this was in the vicinity of 1885 when it happened in Kinigunan a family named Tovuti, I did not witness it but the full detail was given to me, and in those day I could speak the native language fluently, I was told if I spoke and nobody knew who it was they thought it was a native speaking, in many occasion I have surprised natives too.

Adultery in New Britain specially in Kinigunan is a rather unfair offence, in this way that an innocent person has to suffer for the misdeed of a couple.

When a husband find his wife commiting that offence, he ask no question, he simply arm himself and the first unfortunate person he meet he simply let him have it, either it is a kill or a wound, if the victim is of an important family God help the culprit, the relations of the victim take it out of the relations of the culprit in blood and diwara, fortunately diwara, as it seems more important than human being, this may end in a fight or it is settled by paying a price if it turn out to a fight and the woman has no support from her side she generally was killed and send to the next neighbor to be eaten, for this the neighbor pay ten or twenty diwara, if she is from a strong family she is safe because her people will save her.

To my knowledge there is no recognized king or Chief, the authority only go as far as the head of the family, and the strongest and richest has a little more say in the matter, and is recognized as the chief of a district but has no power to command nor to punish, he has the same right as the head of any family in his district, for this reason there is no such a thing as a great chief behind the district, and the whole district is comprised of villages of about ten to twenty huts the next village may be half mile away, in case of a fight the women clear away and hide and the men come together, generally the fight last until one is wounded or killed then the fight is ended, until the victim is revenged on some other occasion, in any fight I never seen more than one or two wounded or killed, it often occur that the relation of the victim turn against the instigator of the fight, unless the party is very strong in his family it may turn out very bad for the starter, it was a good thing for me knowing their weakness I made use of it to protect myself.

The natives of New Britain are cultivators each has his taro patch the village as a rule is situated amongst cocosnut palms, the garden may be one or three miles away, it is the usual method to change the patch each year, they never plant twice the same patch one after another, when the last of the produce is collected they abandon it.

It is a rule that they leave a patch cultivated until the last plant is collected, this turn out to be bananas, then they leave this patch for perhaps three or four years, every season they make a new patch as near as possible to the old one, on account of carting the shoots from the old garden to the new one, a taro plant has about six shoots that is six taros plants for the new patch.

The mode of clearing the patch is as follow, the men cut the undergrowth and let it dry then burn it, after that if there is any large trees they only ringbark it they only cut the small trees, after the fire has done its work, the women come and clear the ground of all rubish make the land ready for planting.

Taros are planted by the men, this is done with a stick of about five feet long of about two and a half inch in diameter made of wild lemon trees or any hard wood trees, they sharpen one end of the stick, and with this they drive the stick in the ground to about a foot deep with a rotary motion which leave a hole of about one foot at the top the rotary movement serve also to loosen the ground around the hole, then the taro shoot is put in the hole with just a little ground around the bottom the hole is never filled to the top only a little is let in to cover the root. Yams is also planted by the men but also by the women, sweet potatoes not very much, bananas sugar cane, maize and quite a lot of variety of plants used for their food, I may state that maize has only been introduced lately, when I arrived in New Britain I never saw any. As a rule the whole family work at the garden, with the exception of small boys who only help of their own accord, during the growing of the garden the weeding is done by the women, the men only collect the produce when ripe, it is the work of the men to dig out the taros and the women to carry it.

When I first arrived the native used grass land in preference because it was easy to work, they use to hoe the ground with a piece of flat stick made of wild palm trees, the men digged and the women cleaned the roots, the grass called alang alang has a long tough white root and require a great deal of handling to get rid of it.

In Kinigunan the natives plant taros and yams, on the North coast where the soil is not so good the native plant bananas of a a special specie for cooking purpose, this banana seems to grow well in pumice stone land, I tried at Kinigunan but was not successful, I suppose nature has provided for those who are living in poor soil.

This is a society the head of a duk duk is called Tubuan an bear the name of the mother's owner, the owner of the Tubuan is a well-to-do man and head of a good family, the tubuan dress is only made of ratan leave and the head is made in the form of a sugar loaf shape, with eyes and mouth painted the height of the head is about two feet from shoulder to top, the dukduk is made of the same pattern only it has a long top gear of about five feet high and has a different face, the dukduk is only periodic but the Tubuan remain the main body of the whole society, any chief or well-to-do man can be the owner of a tubuan which he call after his mother, of course he has to have the means to do so and the acknowlegement of the members.

The initiation of the Dukduk is rather painful, first the candidate must pay ten fathom diwara as an entrance fee, then he is brought to the Puipui which is a selected clearing in the jungle not very far from the village this clearing is fenced with native plants and bamboos, in this enclosure there a long house made of grass used as a shelter.

The members of the society are ranged in two rows in this enclosure each holding a stick in the thickness of a walking stick, each row has about ten to fifteen members, the row is about six feet apart and members are spaced just enough to be confortable in their movement, the candidates are then led from the outside and rushed through the rows the members are ready with their stick in the air to let it drop on the candidate, the best chance a candidate has to run as fast as he can to avoid the punishment, after he has managed to go through this ordeal he is a member of the dukduk, sometime a poor unfortunate candidate not smart enough to rush the ordeal come off rather roughly, after the ceremonie there is a feast plenty to eat and they gorge themselves.

The Dukduk feast last about two months, generally at the opening the tubuan and dukduk are on a canoe sometime two or three canoes are paddled along the beach making the usual noise, ho ho ha ho ho ha, while this going on the duk duk keep a balancing movement while the escort keep singing, this performance terminated they return to the Puipui, while it is on the members of the escort generally live at the Puipui, also the candidates.

The first thing the dukduk do is collecting, the tubuan escorted by the dukduks and some members go to each village and dance in front of each hut then he receive a gift of diwara which vary according to the means of the giver, sometime he receive quarter fathom sometime half and even five fathoms is given, the tubuan receive the biggest share but each dukduk receive also their share, this continue until they have gone through all the villages each collection is brought to the puipui, the tubuan owner take charge of his own, the uncle or relation of the dukduk take charge of their own.

The tubuan carrier can be anybody of the members and they change about but the carrier of a dukduk is a new initiate and has to carry the dress all the time until sometimes he can go no further then he has a spell and they may adjourn until next day, they retire to the puipui, very tired, and so it go on, the carriers of the dukduk are those bridegrooms and the collection go to his uncle who brought a wife for him.

No woman is allowed to go to the puipui or call it club, in olden time very often a poor woman had been knocked on the head for the misfortune of meeting the tubuan in the road, when a woman meet the dukduk who is generally well announced by the noise they made with ho ho ha they have time to rush into the shrub and hide until the escort is over. The Dukduk society is very useful in its power, for instance it can be used to collect debts, this is called ukaukap and the proceeding is as follow, the creditor take with some betel nuts on a leaf of banana together with five or more diwara, present himself to the club and mention so naming the name owe me say twenty fathoms diwara for mention the reason, and I want you to collect it.

The members of the dukduk, may be twenty or fifty, go to

the debtor's hut and stay there until they have collected the money, and while they are there they use all the belonging of the the debtor such as food poultry etc, while some are waiting some of them go to the debtor's taro patch and help themselve with what they need and cook in the village, in such case the village is deserted, so the longer the debtor wait the worse he will get so as a rule a few hours settle the matter, the members bring the collected debt to the creditor, it also square some of the unfair claims, I take it that the dukduk is actually taking the place of the police, a claim can be made while the dukduk is not open the proceeding is to go to the owner of the tubuan and state the case then he will fix a day for the members to meet at the club, the claimant must not forget to shout a good feast that is comprised of fish and taro smeared with the cocosnut cream, this is prepared in this manner, the fish is cooked on hot stone in lieu of fish fowl can be used, the taro is roasted in the fire and it is cooking stones are in the fire to be heated, then while this going on a cup is made of wild banana leafs in such way that it act as a basin, in this the milk of the cocosnut which is squeezed from the scraped kernel, this milk is mixed with a certain leaf of a tree the leaf is rubbed into the milk, without this leaf the milk will not turn into cream. The stones are now red hot and are fastened by the string made of the stem of wild banana leafes, each stone is then dropped gently into the milk the result of this proceeding is that the milk turn into a thick frosty cream, the cream is then poured on the fish and taro who have been open with a little bamboo stick, this dish is called aku, and is not bad at all when I knew the secret of the leaf many time I have had the same dish. The members are then served on banana leafs which takes the place of plate, after the first meal the rest is left to the members who have all they need from the guilty party. I have been initiated into the dukduk and it has helped me a great deal in my dealing with the natives, the difference was that the chief who took me stood over me and the stick did not come down on me. In one instance I had the opportunity to have recourse to the ukaukap some of the natives made a breach of contract with me then to punish them I brought ten fathom diwara and I wanted thirty fathoms for myself and the rest would be theirs, I got my thirty fathom alright but they claimed fifty.

Burial: the body is propped against some support generally a drum or a tree, then he is decorated with all his ornaments such as opossum teeth collar, his diwara collar, and he is painted with stripes of red, white and yellow, and feathers on his head, at the call of the drum, the spectators appear and a great crowd arrive to witness the burial, the mourners distribute the usual betel nut, each spectator take just a couple and proceed to chew it, another mourner follow and give to each spectator a piece of diwara it may be from a quarter fathom to two or three, according to the importance of the man, while this is going on the women all painted black are crying for all they worth, it is not crying it is howling, after the spectators have received their little donation, then the body is stripped of all the ornaments of value, rolled in a mat and burried, the burial ground is next to the hut and sometime in the hut itself, the natives are using the village for that purpose they have no special allotment for cemetery, after that all the spectators leave for their own home, some of the mourner women make a fire on the grave and keep howling for a considerable time sometime days, of course they are paid to do it.

The fire is kept going for a length of time varying from one month to two months, mourning is kept up by the men blackening their faces with charcoal, women burning a round nut the shape of a walnut, I do not know the name, this nut give a greasy black this they smear over their faces and hair, the mourning duration last for some time six months some time longer.

The next of kin is the nephew the son of the dead sister, if he has a son or daughter they are not the heirs and are not entitled to anything, in this case we presume that the deceased was an eagle totem all his children would be hawk totem, and the children of his sister would be eagle totem and are the heirs, the older of the family generally keep the lot, if he has no nephew it go to his brother, if he has no brother well they find someone who take the lot amongst the eagle totem.

The natives are very superstitious, they do not believe in natural death they believe that he has been poisoned by an enemie or cursed by somebody, one of their ways of punishing the culprit at Kinigunan was to cut the little finger from the corpse and send it to Kerawara Duke of York Islands who had the reputation to be able to revenge the deceased, this was done by burning the finger and the smoke from the fire would reach the culprit and he would die sooner or later, on some other occasion they blame some of the neighbors, and if by coincidence the poor devil they suspect should become ill or die, he was the man all right who caused the trouble. They also are great believers in the power of their tribe to be able to poison a person by simply blowing the poison toward their victim, also by just putting the poison with a stick the size of a match, the effect of this superstition is that the fellow who has such reputation make use of it to his advantage, though the result is only imagination, my experience in this matter is that the only poison they have is extracted from plants, and in this case is a matter of swallowing, I have offered ten fathom diwara to such a reputable man using very secret communication, all I got out of it was that I found out that he was a fraud, and he knew it himself so he would not accept my gift as long as I did not make it public, there was no reason for him to be uneasy about that, no native would believe me if I did.

On one occasion a chief has been ill for a considerable time, and at his convalescence it was judged necessary by his people that he should be nurished with human flesh, at least a feast of human flesh would restore his health, therefore a victim had to be procured and this victim must be from a neighbor village, this is how it was arranged. A black sheep of the family was picked out, a boy of about twenty or less, too old would not be so tender, a price is offered to the boy's relatives perhaps twenty fathom diwara or less, then a day is fixed the relatives lead the boy to an ambush on some excuse of some sort, when he reach the spot agreed upon the purchasers fall on him and kill him, and the victim is carried to his destination to be eaten, this all has been done in the quiet, the sole rememberance about the disappearance is that he is gone and a good riddance he must have been taken by the Devil called akai an imaginary spirit in the same way as we have the devil, the natives do not believe in good spirits there is only one to be feared and it is the one who can do harm.

They also attach great importance if an individual is sick, the occupants of the hut where he sleep must not sleep anywhere else while he is sick, should one do so it is sure to make him worse, this is called vakubak.

If by misfortune a native canoe is carried away to sea by the current and he or they should reach the beach at some other district, they are considered victims of the sea and on such ground are killed and of course it is another excuse for a feast.

A bushman going to sea for the first time has to pay a penalty, in Kinigunan the penalty was rather cruel, on the ground that he has gone to sea for the first time, the beach tribe kill or wound some of their own tribe or a neighbor and the poor fellow has to pay the pot, this is one of their unjust customs, in the north coast in such case they are more generous instead of killing and causing an unjust act they force the noviciate to shout, and the whole matter finish by a good feast at the expense of the fellow.

They have Ingiet that is a kind of a pledge that the members will not eat pork, there is no punishment if they break the pledge but the superstition keep them from doing so, it is of no value and it only affect those who have taken the pledge.

Tawal the natives contrary to our fashion like to have their teeth black, this is done by some mineral collected from the vulcan, this is kept on the teeth, while this performance is going on the patient eat very little and he keep in a unmarried people's hut that would be the bachelor hut, until the teeth are black it take some time a couple weeks, generally when the patient come out he look rather as if he could do with a good feed, but having his teeth black make him proud.

The Mission bought a small yacht from Sydney and were good enough to let me have it, so we went to New Hanover and along the coast of New Ireland, but owing to the fact that there was a Frenchman established at Kung I made for it thinking that with his help I would get good recruits, but it turned out a failure, we only stayed a couple of days and had to turn back very disapointed, Gangloff the Frenchman an escapee from New Caledonia[83] came with us as far as Kavieng and we left him there where he had business.

Having already wasted some time unsuccessfully disgusted we returned and I did not even try, my aim was to get home as quick as possible. However I had a bit of luck as we were keeping close to the shore of New Ireland I saw a lot of natives making signs waving, so we made for the shore and sure enough I made a good haul I got nearly twenty boys within a few hours, and since then this place called Ratubu has supplied me with labourers, as I did not like to lose my luck no sooner the recruits were on board that we started from there to Kinigunan it was only

[83] For a portrait of Casimir Gangloff see Cayley-Webster (1898: 289-93). In 1891 he lost his right arm and eye in a dynamite explosion but this did not stop him from being a 'veritable Brigham Young' and having 'many wives, principally natives of New Hanover'.

forty miles so we were at Kinigunan in the early morning. At that time I shifted my house from the beach to about 300 yards further inland on a little hill where it is yet, I had at that time a Frenchman who did the carpentering with my help when I could, we managed to have the house transferred I made it higher by splicing two feet off the stanchion of one room to make the difference the point in those days was to do with the material on hand.

While this was going on there was a Greek who had a small vessel which I brought from him, the 'Magnetic' this I used for trading but unfortunately she was too small to do any good, and she finished by smashing herself on the shore of New Ireland. All this time I was keeping my plantation going slowly as my means permitted.

About a little after I had my house shifted I think it must be in 1893 the natives became restless and rumours were circulating that the natives would chase the whitemen and take their land again, of course knowing their language I was kept in touch with all the rumours to make things worse they had a fanatic who made them believe that he had invented a mixture if rubbed over the body would make a man unvulnerable, no harm could reach the person so smeared, this was only a kind of ointment made of cocosnut oil mixed with some leafs crushed together and the usual cantation over it. The natives believing in such power become very beligerent, rumours circulated of a trial made by them of shot being fired at a man and the bullet did not effect him, with this belief the natives became very abusive, even came to the New Guinea Company plantation and started to pull out the cotton plants, but the police boys soon send them away, no doubt the password was given on my side I found out tracks of many natives just about quarter of a mile from my house and the ground very much tramped, this was a sure sign that if they had succeeded with the New Guinea Company at Kokopo they were ready to attack me, fortunately a few shots dispersed them and the attempt failed.

The New Guinea Company was a German Chartered Company who acted as Government as well, Kolbe[84] was the business

<hr>

[84] Comment on the margin: 'Big fellow fair not handsome'. August Karl Paul Kolbe was a former Prussian cavalry officer who had come out to the police service of the New Guinea Company. He lost his job in December 1893

administrator as well as the Government magistrate, Geisler was in charge of the plantation the native police were under a German exsoldier who drilled them and controlled the whole force, I should think the force of the police at that time was about fifty men, this was not very much of a force but with the help of a German Man-of-war it was quite sufficient. The next day after the attack by the natives it was decided by the head of the Company and staff to punish the natives of the village where the rumours circulated from, knowing that I could give them help with my knowledge of native I was of the party.

At the time there was a German Man-of-war in port,[85] so it was agreed in conjunction to punish the natives. On the appointed day which was only a couple days after the attack we started from Kokopo at ten p.m. so as to be ready at the break of day-light, Kolbe, Geisler, myself and the Officer in charge of the native police, also some of the friendly natives who were only few and served as guides under me.

We slept near the village and during the night the natives send stones at us with their slings, which did not do any harm, at daylight we make a move on, our greatest trouble against us was the narrow path only one at a time could walk right and left thick jungle and some part of it prickly, in such disadvantage we had to move on, the natives could see us but we could not, our progress was very slow and the surroundings very still the only

---

as a result of 'disciplinary proceedings', almost certainly because of his role in the 1893 uprising and, being not only unemployed but also in debt, he proposed to Queen Emma and was accepted (after Farrell's death, in 1886, she lived with Captain Agostino Stalio but he was killed in 1892). The couple died in Monte Carlo in 1913, within two days of each other.

[85] The cruiser *Sperber*, captained by von Arnoldi, which arrived in New Guinea early in December 1893. The 'expeditionary' force consisted of the local contingent mentioned by Mouton, in charge of Kolbe, and a group of sixty sailors from the *Sperber*, led by the Administrator Schmiele. According to the French version (p. 73), on the eve of the punitive expedition the villagers had offered Mouton *diwara* on the condition that he did not join it, but he said he was a 'Whiteman' and had to go with the others. Mouton also fails to mention the shelling of the rebellious villagers, possibly because it was ineffective. The uprising, which lasted from March until December 1893, was caused by Queen Emma's encroachment on village land and was triggered off by the behaviour of her Buka labourers. There was an earlier attack on Ralum in March 1890.

sound was the birds, then of a sudden as we reached a bunch of bamboo the fun started, bullets stones started, no spears the distance was not suitable for spear throwing, we returned the fire, but the natives no sooner firing that they disappeared toward an elevated village called Mukuravudu, we could hear them at some distance and now again a stone or two would reach us to show us that they were there, from the guide I become aware of their tactic, when we reached a grass patch they showed fight again and their intention was to rush us, but our fire kept them out, we could have done a lot of damage if the native police had been more disciplined, but it was no use they fired at anything, it was at that patch that I managed to drop a fellow with white feathers on his head and a round disk on his chest he was about three hundred yards, all I can say is that we saw him drop and the next the blood, the wounded was carried away.

Later we arrived at a village on a hill there the natives came from all directions uphill to attack us with the exception of one side which showed level ground the rest could not be approached by climbing to reach us, the native police were uncontrolable and I and the officer and the other whites told them not to use our amunition wastefully, the natives came from all directions, at last through the level side we saw a fellow painted red and white and carrying no arms all he had in each hand a bunch of croton like a bunch of flowers, he did not last long as soon seen he was shot, from that moment we could have heard a pin drop after a while, no sooner the wizard dropped all we could hear was the rush of natives through the bush, I cut one of his ears to show the natives of Kinigunan, so that the fact that they really believed the wizard and evidently he believed it himself because he was unarmed and like a priest leading his followers, this part of the attack only concerned those of that village or district we had to pass through some other districts who did not know the death of the wizard so we had to be careful to go back we had two roads the nearest we had to cross a river not very wide but each side very steep, my guide informed me that it was quite possible for the enemies to drop rocks from the top, that was enough for me I took the longer road but we missed the ambush, but on the other hand we were not expected to return that way and Parkinson told the Man-of-war sailors who were watching that the enemies would come the way we did, we did not know nothing about this arrangement and the first thing we heard when we come to the open was a shot as it come from a pistol it sounded very much like a native shot, so we shot at the smoke and I and Geisler who were pretty good shots caused a stir and then the sailors send their volley, we soon knew that it was not native fire it was fortunate for us that where we were there was a sloping ground which we used quick and lively, and had we been on level ground I am afraid that we would have fared very badly.

Fortunately we only fired two shots, the native police did not shoot for a wonder they obeyed, the sailors after having send a couple of volleys become to wonder and stopped firing and as we did not fire the silence reigned and my whistle could be heard and shout, so we managed to reach the sailors unscratched, of the fight the only damage we had is a friendly native shot through the arm and only a flesh wound no bone broken, and a few bullet holes through native loincloth called lavalava, of the enemie we shot a few but not many two we were sure the natives did not like to admit their defeat. The death of the witch or wizard settled the whole matter to a certain point,[86] for instance when I show my natives the ear they told me that it was the ear of a child, so we were rather on the alert, some of the natives kept showing troublesome, they would set fire to grass pull cotton plants and show very insolent yet, as it was with the ear it did not suit them to believe, I could see by their eyes that there was something brewing.

My friend Togua told me that there was a plot to wipe out Kokopo, that is the New Guinea Company the plan was to get the firearms and then take the rest would be easy, unfortunately for them they did not estimate the reverse, the back of my place where there was a track going to Kokopo showed to me that a great number of natives had used the path, also one day I noticed a lot of natives hiding about three hundred yards from my house in the shrub, while some were busy with Kokopo they would attack me and no doubt the Mission also, but I must say that it

---

[86] The 'wizard's' name was Tavalai. He belonged to the Paparatava and had reportedly received 1000 fathoms *diwara* for his ointment. Salisbury (1970: 80) gives the native account of the reason for the uprising's failure: one of the local converts to Methodism obtained some of the magic ointment and gave it to the Government forces thus making them invulnerable. Mouton's assertion that the 'death of the wizard settled the whole matter to a certain point' is equally plausible, however.

was only their way of looking at the position, and the remaining belief of the witch, fortunately their first attempt was a failure at once and lasted only one day, then matters became normal again and by that time the news that the witch was really killed by a bullet convinced them that the witch was a fraud, meanwhile the witch must have done well because I understand that he sold his medicine for diwara, by what I can gather is that, with the complicity of some fellow from the village he made a business of this fraud for some time before it came to a head, and the rumours about shooting came only from the same village, of course I presume that he only used blank cartridges or loaded the gun but omitted the bullet, it is wonderful how such a simple trick could cause a lot of trouble, what I cannot understand is that the witch who was a young man of no more than twenty five or thirty years old, must have believed the fraud himself, the indication of such belief is that he approached us unarmed and was dancing and singing and in such way that showed that he was not afraid of bullet.

Just about a little after this occurence I came to the conclusion that if I could get a little capital I would be able to get along so I approached the New Guinea Company for a loan of one thousand pound, they were willing to do so at the rate of eight per cent, but meantime Father Couppé[87] the head of the Sacred Heart Mission in New Britain made me an offer to lend me the money for ten years at the rate of five per cent, I understand that Father Couppé heard from someone that I had approached the New Guinea Company, so I accepted the offer, against my land as security, that is about three thousand acres of land, and some of it planted with cocosnut trees a good weatherboard house etc.

After having borrowed the money I came to the conclusion that the best thing for me was to be independent, I started to get my goods from Sydney Father Merg then Procurator for the Mission acted as Agent, I kept on little by little I sold my copra to Burns Philp & Co. Ltd.[88] of Sydney and ordered goods from

[87] Bishop, not Father Couppé (see fn. 79).

[88] Established in 1883 by the amalgamation of the various business interests of James Burns and Robert Philp, the firm ran a subsidised shipping service to British New Guinea from 1886. The line was extended to German New Guinea in 1898 but Burns Philp was driven out of the Protectorate in 1905. The correct name of the firm is Burns, Philp and Co.

Sydney, in this manner I got my goods cheaper and got a better price for a produce, the SS 'Moresby' was then running Captain Williams as Master.

In 1896 or thereabout a german named Deckner came to me and I employed him as overseer in the plantation and a help as well, he came to the territory with a crowd of gold miners who bought a small boat the 'Strella' with the intention of prospecting for gold, but they were disappointed, the New Guinea Company Government did want any gold mining business going on for time being so they had to give it up,[89] they tried trading in shells but it did not pay, so two of the crew both Germans stayed Deckner and Schneider, Deckner stayed with me and the other went with the New Guinea Company.[90]

Deckner was a dreamer he told me that there was a good thing in the Admiralty Islands in beachlemer [*bêche-de-mer*], and asked if I would finance the scheme which was to go to Sydney by a small schooner of about 25 tons or thirty. The idea was rather risky he himself was not a sailor and had no ticket however he learned how to take the sun and he was able to the sextant, and even he could overcome the trouble by engaging a master with a certificate to bring the ship in, we agree and I gave instructions to my Agent to supply the funds, I paid his passage on the 'Moresby' to Sydney, he did not waste time in Sydney he was lucky to find a small schooner of twenty five tons fitted her and sailed from Sydney as far as I can remember he picked up a crew enough to handle the ship and one day he sailed away without troubling about the shipping law, however his departure was not noticed, and the New Guinea Company Government did not trouble about it in those days they were not so particular. He was very lucky to have fine weather and made a very good passage I think he only took twenty two days to reach Kokopo.

We paid off the crew and replaced them by native crew, his first trip was for the Admiralty, and filled the vessel with beachlemer of all mixed quality, while at the Admiralty Islands he got rather a scare he was surrounded by canoes and he did not like the attitude of the natives, the natives of the Admiralty were

[89] The story of the search for gold in the territory (including the German period) has been told in Healy 1965. Also useful is Blum (1900: 140-46).

[90] 'Returned to' would be more appropriate: Schneider was earlier (in 1889-90) captain of the company's ship *Ysabel*.

known to be very bellicose but he managed to make a paying trip, the conditions were that the ship would be his when he could pay off what it cost, unfortunately he did not see his way clear to make a second trip to the Admiralty. The native name for the Admiralty is Manus so that the enterprise as far as Deckner was concerned ended, then he went for green snails, at St. John Islands there he established his business with the natives but there again he brought a load of green snails shells and did not feel inclined to collect the fruit of his enterprise, the vessel was in his name but mortgaged to me so I had to take the vessel from him. A chinaman went a few months after and made a good haul of green snail shell which should have been Deckner's if he only went a second time for it and really collect the fruit of his organisation.

In 1897 Captain Monrad and Captain Rondahl[91] and myself we formed a partnership for the purpose of establishing trading stations all over the territory, under the name of O. Mouton & Co. Captain Monrad was a danish national Captain Rondahl a swede and I Belgian, to have the vessel under one flag we arranged to be naturalized Germans.

Captain Rondahl and Monrad went to Sydney and purchased a ketch of forty five tons, they filled her with cargo and returned to Kokopo, my place was only half mile from Kokopo.

The Ship's name was 'Muruna' she was build at Narooma, and was about 50 tons gross, Captain Monrad took charge of her, the first trip she made was to Ontong Java (Lord Howe Islands) not the Lord Howe known by Sydney people only a few mile from Sydney, there we established a trader but could not obtain any land the natives would not sell land, so we used a native to do the trading under the supervision of the King Weela,[92] then after that we went to Greenwich Islands one degree

[91] Comment on the margin: 'He married Grace Coe. He divorced her, she married Schmidt who was working on [his] plantation [Kabakaul]. He then worked the plantation for Rondahl. Grace a very fine woman.' Walter Schmidt later owned Rainau plantation.
[92] Spelt Uila in Sarfert and Damm (1929: 8). The first copra trader on the island was a Samoan who worked for Queen Emma in the early 1890s, also under the auspices of King Uila. Hernsheim followed soon after and Mouton around 1897. Both established themselves on Luangiua where most of the 3000 or so islanders lived. Hernsheim withdrew after the islands were transferred to Great Britain as a result of the Samoa Treaty of 1899, and Mouton ceased to trade there in 1903. Queen Emma's trader remained on the islands until 1909 after which date Lever Bros had a monopoly of the local copra trade.

north of the equator, on this Island there was already one named Patterson who traded for Mrs. Forsayth,[93] the Captain took him to Ponape, the Spanish Government gave us proper permit to trade at Greenwich Islands Mrs. Forsayth did not get that permit and was trading on the Island without any permit, here I must explain that Mrs. Forsayth was Mrs. Farrell previously mentioned, she took Farrell's business on hand after his death, she [*Muruna*] brought some copra with her from Greenwich, the next trip was to put trader on Gardner Island,[94] Kavieng New Ireland, then the 'Muruna' made a trip to Manus and brought a load of beachlemer.

When we could spare the 'Muruna' we used her recruiting, the first trip we had a good luck we took more then she could take the recruits swimed on board, this batch was for a term of three years, I was very pleased to have them for my plantation.

The plantation was my own private property and was not included in the company, the company interests were only concentrated on the outside business, even the store was my own which I supplied to the company at cost price, we kept going for a while the three of us then Rondahl showed some lack of interest in the business, and after one year we dissolved partnership and only Monrad and I remained together, Rondahl started a plantation at Kulon or rather Mrs. Rondahl did, she was the capable pioneer, Rondahl would not have had much if it has not been for her Mrs. Rondahl was related to Mrs. Forsayth.

Then I and Monrad were together, and I must say that we agree very well together, often my first contingent of labourers finished their time we had to return them to their place at Bougainville, after three years each recruit had a box filled with sundry trade goods such as tobacco pipes axes butcher knives beads printed calico to the value of what was due to them.[95] The

[93] Louis Patterson, an Englishman who settled on the islands in 1892 and married the daughter of a local 'high priest'. He died in 1899 (Emory 1965: 17). For Mrs Forsayth substitute Mrs Kolbe: she married Kolbe in 1893 (see fn. 84) but traded under the name E. E. Forsayth.

[94] Also known as Tabar. In 1893 Mouton had recruited thirty labourers on the island (French version, p. 77).

[95] The usual monthly wage of an indentured plantation worker was five marks, plus food and lodgings. As a rule this was supplemented by a weekly issue of one or two sticks of tobacco and a box of matches, and a monthly issue of a *lavalava* and perhaps a clay pipe a well. A blanket, a bowl and a spoon, issued

landing was not always a pleasant business, some time it was more dangerous than recruiting, in some instance we had to be very careful to land the boys in their proper village, if not a mistake would mean the death of the boy for the sake of the goods and would also serve as a feast menus for the crowd I am now speaking of 1900.

While we returned the laborers we also wanted new recruits, in one instance while we were returning and recruiting in Bougainville, of course I did the recruiting while the Captain remained on board to look after the ship, that day in the morning early seeing a lot of natives on shore I went on shore and by the look of things there was a good prospect, I had New Britain boys with me to guard against any trouble, on land at one place at mouth of a creek where the crowd of natives were standing, I notice some queer movement on the part of one or two natives, and in kanaka language I gave instruction to my guard to be prepared, I noticed for one thing, that a native made a very funny movement in coming toward the boat, he seemed to walk dragging something, and another one came near the boat with one of his arms kept close to his body, like if he was keeping something under his arm, I also noticed a peculiar glitter in his eyes, so when I thought that he was near enough, I pointed my revolver at him and told him to lift his arms, so sure enough under his dropped a short handled hatchet, and those dragging their feet were dragging spears with their toes, had they been able to be near enough it would have been an attack, the one with the hatchet would knock me on the head and the spears would have come out of the water like lightning, of course I warned my crew of the move which I detected, and we were prepared, my knowledge of the native change of face and the glittering of the eyes gave them away, well a native do not turn white or red but he turn the colour of ash and the eyes give a sparking shade, which jump as well like trembling, however having discovered their deceitful plan, and seeing that it was failure they acted as if

---

on arrival, completed the list of a labourer's worldly possessions. If a worker came from an outlying district the employer usually withheld half of the cash wage; on the expiration of the contract the sum due was converted into trade goods such as those mentioned by Mouton. In 1907 some of Mouton's labourers at Kinigunan were paid ten marks a month (CAO, AA 63/83, box 52, case 10/1907).

nothing has occured and I recruited just as if nothing had happened, in fact after they found out that it was no use, and I told them in a laughing manner turning the whole matter as a joke, exactly what was their plan and action they laughed, and they say that I know too much, that day I did a good recruiting day, though they were prepared to kill me and the crews. The business was doing well in those days it was the time to do well though the price for copra was not much on the Island we got a good price in Sydney, later things changed and we made better conditions to the traders, some of the stations did not do well for instance we had one on Gardner Island and it did not do well, under one manager it would do well and under another one it would do very badly, in the trading business there was always a chance of striking the wrong one.

On one occasion when we came to Gardner Island we found the station empty, the manager had disappeared, we found out that he had sold the copra to some vessel and went to Sydney, some of those traders passing by boat would help them just to get the copra cheap also a plausible story would be accepted.

While I had the 'Muruna' I still had the 'Minna' and this boat was doing some recruiting and loading copra from near stations, after Deckner left I had to get a captain to take charge of her, first I had an old man who had been in Manus doing trading there, and I thought to send him to Manus but he did not like it so after having done some recruiting I had to get rid of him, then I got another one but he did not last long, one day I went with him to take a cargo of copra, during the night a north west blow came and as the anchorage was unsafe the Captain tried to heave anchore and get away, he may have done so if he had been sober, but it was too late the vessel went on shore, and landed nicely on a sandy patch without damage,[96] she was very strongly build of Australia hardwood, her ribs were natural so I had to get rid of the skipper and the vessel remained on shore for twelve months, everthing movable was taken out of her and put at the trader's shed at the time I had a German trading for me.

While the 'Minna' was on shore the 'Muruna' was doing good work, and so far we were doing well, Monrad was the propper man for the business, the 'Muruna' between carting copra and

[96] In December 1900, on the island of Watom (German New Guinea 1900-01).

attending to the traders, had no time to spare and it was quite a strain to have a week to recruit, if we did so it was felt and some trading business had to be neglected, once a year we send the 'Muruna' to Greenwich, on this occasion this trip Monrad went to Greenwich and when he arrived there he found out that the trader Patterson died a few days before he reached the Island, he died of T.B. Monrad made an inventory of the stock on hand with the mate as a witness, and when he came back to Kinigunan I made the A/c and after the stock on hand and produce received, it proved that we were the looser of a few hundred pounds.

About the same year Hersheim and Co. Matupi brought the first auxiliary vessel from San Fancisco, amongst the crew there was an Americanized Weed, he told me that he would be able to save the 'Minna' he tried but failed, then a frenchman who also was a crew of the same ship stayed with me and while with me I kept him busy with sewing sails for boats, then he told me that he would have a try at the 'Minna', so I made arrangement with him that he would have half of the ship's value if I could sell her, after he worked for about one month, he succeeded in saving her and he brought her to Kinigunan, the ship at that time was no use to me so, not very long after, Schneider who was a party of the crew with Deckner came to me and asked if I would sell the 'Minna' this I accepted and the ship was sold to Schneider, I do not remember the price but I think it was about six hundred pounds, I gave Pourteau three hundred pounds as agreed, Pourteau then went to Hernsheim and Co. and made for Hersheim and Co. their plantation at Portland Islands he made a good job of it, and after he had trouble with Hernsheim he started a plantation of his own in the Bainings, later, he was a very capable man. When we started with the partnership there was also another scheme on we had our eyes on French Islands and it was agreed that Peter Hansen[97] then on the Islands would

[97] 'King Peter' Hansen, a Danish sailor with a long association with New Guinea. He had traded for the D.H.P.G. in the early 1880s, accompanied Finsch on his 1884 expedition, joined Queen Emma in 1885 and worked for her in a number of localities, including Ontong Java and Nukumanu. He was the first trader on the French Islands (officially known at Vitu Islands since 1909) which he 'bought' in 1898 for the New Guinea Company, living in a style which became legendary. In 1903 the islanders burned down his house, killed most of his traders and he himself apparently escaped only by accident. He was not allowed to return, and spent the next five years managing planta-

buy from the natives all the land he could, but this turned out a failure, Peter Hansen preferred to deal with the New Guinea Company and left us in the lurch, had he done what we wanted him to do we would have had the French Islands to our asset, and as it proved later a very good one at that, Hansen with the credit of the New Guinea Company lived in high style and finished by losing all he had and died a poor man at Rabaul, I often met him at Rabaul and in talking I told him what a fool he has been but he said he had a good time and he was quite satisfy, so no more about it.

It was about that time 1900-1901 that I could not manage the plantation who was going on splendidly that I engaged a clerk to help me while I was looking after the plantation he was doing all the clerical work and the store, he was Dutch by nationality and a very good reliable man, having somebody in charge of my place, we decided to go to Sydney to have an engine put into the 'Muruna', and in 1902 we started for Sydney[98] on board the 'Muruna', during the trip Captain Monrad had sore eyes and I had to take the observation with the sextant I could take the morning and the evening sun but the noon was rather intriguing so Monrad managed that part, this only last a few days then his eyes got better, from Kinigunan we went to Greenwich Islands to take a load of copra to act as balast, and also to leave Monrad's wife a native from Greenwich on the Island while we went to Sydney, that was the first time I went to Greenwich. We did not get favourable wind and it took us a week to make about four hundred miles, we stayed on the Island a few days to land trade and take copra.

Greenwhich Islands[99] is composed of eleven small Islands all

tions on the Gazelle Peninsula. In 1908 he went to Bougainville to run the Toiemonapu plantation for the New Britain Corporation, established in Sydney in 1907. He died a virtual pauper in Rabaul. (For a detailed biography, see Groves 1925.)

[98] Possibly a slip of memory. According to the French version (pp. 81 and 85) Mouton had visited Sydney in 1900 and again in 1901.

[99] Also known as Kapingamarangi or, to Spanish scientists, as Los Pescadores, the islands had a population of about 150-200 in Mouton's time. The islanders' lack of stamina, referred to below by Mouton, may have been due to ringworm. 'Nearly every native was covered with the skin disease called "tokelan ring-worm" in Fiji,' said the Captain of H.M.S. *Espiègle* in 1883 (Eilers 1934: 6).

covered with cocosnut palms, they are very flat Islands, and the natives depend on cocosnuts and breadfruits for their diet also a gunagun a small taro growing in brakish water, the breadfruits is preserved by the natives, they use the ripe fruits which they roll in a thin sheet and then they roll it like a sausage, or to be more accurate like the sailors do with tobacco leafes, they make a paste of it and dry it in the sun with a roller they press it as fine as they can, and roll it as tight as possible then they cover it with pandanus leaves, they are some of them as long as four feet and of about three inches diameter the taste is not unlike fig.

The Islands are atoles fringing on one side by the eleven Islands so near each other that a low tide one can walk from one to the other, on one side are the Islands and the rest is fringed by reefs this form practically a large cup the inside is the lagoon which in some place is deep enough to take the largest ship, the appearance is very pretty, the lagoon is about two miles long perhaps more, the white bottom sand give the water a sky blue, the Islands are fringed with cocosnut palms and the green against the white beach and blue water resemble the picture the Japanese are so fond of painting, the inside of each Island is generally reserved for bread-fruit trees, the whole Islands if the natives did not use such a lot for their food would produce about 100 tons of copra, but it is a good year if they produce 50 tons, and some year when the drought is on they cannot spare any it has to be used for food, their principal food is fish and cocosnut the bread-fruit rolls they make are kept for emergencie when the drought is on, there is only one small passage to enter the lagoon and it is necessary to go in at hight tide or when the tide come in so that the current help to go in, I dont suppose that the entrance is more than hundred feet and at some place less, in going in one can see the coral reef on each side of the vessel.

The natives are the same as in the Carolines they are copper colour some of them quite light, and the girls are rather good to look at, the physique is rather fair size in the men some of them

---

The same was true twenty-five years later (Eilers 1934: 56; Schlaginhaufen 1908: 955). Monrad was well-known on the islands as Captain 'Monera' and had introduced the sweet potato there (Eilers 1934: 149).

are six feet high and strongly build, only they have no stamina in them, their life is too easy to give them enough excercise to make them hard, when loading copra it is a point not to fill the bag too full, I doubt if they could carry a bag of about 120 pounds, they may for a short while but not long.

The men's duty is to fish and to get cocosnuts and if they make copra to cut and dry the nut in the sun, they generally split the nut in two after the fibre husk has been removed and expose the kernel to the sun, at night they turn the nuts upside down so as to expose the shell to the rain if any, this make very good copra when there is fine weather in three days the nuts are dried beautifully white, this is cut in three or five pieces and stored into the shed ready to be bagged when the ship come, the women are doing all the cooking and some of them are very clever in making hats made of pandanus leafes, they are so well done that they are the shapes of panama hats, they are also good at making fine mats, and some of them are so well done and soft that the women use them as a loin cloth, like everywhere else amongst the pacific the women have the worst end of the stick, but in Greenwich Islands they cannot complain they have a very easy time.

Their life is very calm and simple, they are even so calm that I do not think that they have a row amongst themselves, theft is not known they have only spear for fish as a weapon, for fish not for fighting, as they have no enemies, their nearest neighbor is miles away no less than three hundred miles of pacific ocean separate them. However in the past they have had visitors long time ago, a canoe landed on Greenwich they were castaways and drifted there all nearly dead from exposure and hunger, the Greenwich natives brought them to life again and kept them for a considerable time, by the description of the natives they must have been natives from the Gilbert Islands, their canoe was a large one and they were no more than six or eight peoples. Those castaways after a while they become homesick and for this purpose made ready with provisions and made their canoe fit for travelling and one day to the surprise of the Greenwich natives they massacred a great number of the Greenwich natives, to that extent that the Island was depleted of their peoples only a few remained, then they took to sea, if the weather was fine and smooth no doubt they reached their goal but otherwise they had to make nine hundred miles to reach their destination, of course they may have reached the nearer Islands.

This is the only tragedy they ever had,[100] but their most fear is drought to them it mean nearly starvation if it last too long, religion I understand that they have a hut reserved in some place which they respect very much, and are talking of a very old man who was the founder of the Islands, I also know that there is one Island without cocosnuts and the natives are very superstitious about it, however like the rest of them they believe in bad spirits.

Having loaded our ship with copra after a stay of one week we made a start and we took with us a couple of Greenwich Islanders as crew, the weather remained rather fine all the time, and from Greenwich to near Newcastle we had very good weather then we caught a nasty southerly bust, and for two days we had to battle against it, this unfortunately put us back two days, the only incident during the trip is that Monrad got bad eye rheumatism in the eyes, so he taught me how to take the sun with the sextant and so we managed.

We arrived in Sydney harbour in May, I know that I had only white suit and I wore two suit to keep me warm, from the time I arrived to the Islands to the time I arrived in Sydney it was twenty one years since I saw civilisation, I think we arrived on a Sunday because it was very quiet, and we could not get in touch with store, the only one we saw was the custom officer who stayed on board to see that we had no dutiable goods on board, beside the customs and the Doctor of course, the only person we came in contact was Paul the butcher in those day he used to to row a skiff to the ship and take orders, Paul was of German descent I believe, the next day business looked brighter that is what make me think that it was a Sunday, Paul was good enough to take me to David Jones and there we got a rig-out complete, Monrad had European clothes but he got a rig-out as well, of course they were ready made clothes, and they were blue serge, I never will forget that day, when I went on shore the noise and the traffic affected me very much, and I was quite useless in the street, this lasted only a few days then I got my nerves quiten and in not time I was O.K. the only thing I could not get out of my imagination is that I had the impression that everybody was looking at

[100] Not altogether correct. According to oral tradition the islands had also been raided by the Madjuro people from the Marshall Islands (Eilers 1934: 150).

me, I know that it was only imagination but there it was and it made me very miserable for a time, until I managed to master this feeling, my friends told me that it was my own imagination and that the people did not take no special notice of me, I just fancy that a man from the outback when he come to the city he must feel like that, and no doubt it is one of the reasons that we can detect a county dweller from a city one, the way he walk and the way he turn round to look if somebody really take notice of him, but he has one thing I did not have and that is the bushman walk, the long and dragging walk.

We gave ourselve a week holiday before we started business, and I think we deserved it, the first thing I had to do was to look for an hotel, W. Lucas[101] of Burns Philp & Co. Ltd. managed that for me and he put me to the Oxford Hotel in King Street, Lucas thought that it would be the best Hotel for me he was right in a way but I did not like it there was something that did not agree with me, what it was I could not tell.

However I did not stay long in a Hotel I did not feel at home so I shifted to the Grand Central in Clarence Street this seemed to suit me better, thought there was not much difference, but I presume that in the Oxford there was some stiffness which I did not like.

Now for business, on inquiries and experts statements we were told that the 'Muruna' was not build for a propeller having no stern post sufficiently large and strong enough to take the propeller, they could do so if we wanted at the expense of the strength of the ship it mean that they would have had to splice a stern post to the original which was one piece keel job, this splicing would weaken the ship and the expenses were to be taken in consideration the quotation was rather heavy, so taking all in consideration we agree that the only thing to do was to go back to Kinigunan and see that what can be done in the matter.

Monrad went back with the 'Muruna' and I went with the 'Moresby' to Kinigunan, quite a civilized citizen, Monrad

[101] Walter H. Lucas joined Burns, Philp and Co. in 1896 and became Islands Inspector in 1910. He was one of the Royal Commissioners on the future of German New Guinea (1919) and, after his resignation from Burns Philp, was appointed chairman of the Expropriation Board. He was said to be a 'most objectionable type of man' whom 'they all hate and are ashamed of' (Bassett 1969: 15 and 38). He left New Guinea in 1927 and died in Canberra in 1954.

arrived at Kinigunan a little behind me but we were not very much far apart to our arrival. After about nine months we talked the matter over again and we decided to have a new schooner build with a engine as auxiliary, therefore I came to Sydney by myself and with the help of Edward Lanser I found the builder of the 'Muruna', who was at Narooma on the south coast, I made all the arrangements and Moat the builder started to work, I made arrangements with Lanser about fixing financial matters and I went away then Lanser kept me informed as the work progressed, in those days I did not know anybody in Sydney and was not too keen on staying in Sydney the sooner I could get away the better for me, so I only paid my visit as the business on hand required, and between the laying of the keel and the finishing touch I only came once to Sydney, the building of the vessel lasted I think nine or twelve months, the 'Muruna' would be in our hand then so we were fortunate enough to sell her to Wahlen[102] for £500 we had no use for her now and it was a fair price we thought, and it was a very useful opportunity to get rid of her, however, Monrad felt it very much to part with his old ship. We received information that the vessel was ready to be launched so we took passage on the 'Moresby' and went to Sydney me and Monrad. On arrival at Sydney we stayed at the Grand Central we had a good room No. 7 with two beds one for Monrad and one for me it was a very good large room and we were able to invite friends to have a drink with us in our room,

[102] Heinrich Rudolph Wahlen came to New Guinea in 1895, at the age of twenty-two. He became an independent trader in 1903, while still a relatively junior clerk with Hernsheim and Co. In 1906 he secured for £5000 from his former employer an option on their Hermit Islands concession, went to Germany where he floated the Heinrich Rudolf Wahlen Aktiengesellschaft and got himself appointed managing director, returned to New Guinea, exercised his option and became almost overnight a man of means. He was appointed Swedish Consul in 1907, owned one of the two first cars on the Gazelle Peninsula (Bishop Couppé had the other) and in 1910 he formed in Germany the Forsayth G.m.b.H. which bought out Queen Emma in the same year (it was converted into the Hamburgische Suedsee-Aktiengesellschaft, or HASAG, in 1913). After 1910 Wahlen spent most of his time in Germany and England (he married the daughter of the Swedish Consul-General in London), and during part of World War One drove a motor ambulance, presented by himself to the German Government. He was still alive in Hamburg in the mid-1960s. His erstwhile employer Eduard Hernsheim died in Germany in 1917.

we stayed quite three months there at that Hotel we could do nothing else than waiting until such time the new 'Muruna' which was called after the old one, was ready to go to sea, the installation of the rigging and the engine took some time, meantime I got married and just a few days before the 'Muruna' left, I remember that the 'Muruna' left in September,[103] me and my wife were staying at the Grand Central at the time, for one thing we had to see the ship off which we did.

From that time to the present day it still remain a secret what has happen, after the departure of the 'Muruna' we left by the 'Moresby' and was surprised to learn that the 'Muruna' did not arrive yet according to time she should have been at Kinigunan a week ago,[104] by the disappearence of the new 'Muruna' a great calamity befel me all our enterprise and prospect came to a standstill, we had made arrangement to tackle the Carolines etc. and many other prospects, now I was left with the whole business in my hand and my right hand gone, I found it impossible to carry on, because Monrad never could be replaced. After allow three months to expire I had to get a vessel to replace the 'Muruna' thought at the time the Norddeutscher Lloyd[105] was a great help because they were taking the copra cargo from every station still my recruiting business would suffer also place where the N.D.L. boats would not go, for instance the N.D.L. went to Greenwich twice and would not go again, on account of the passage, however the passage was allright with a steamer if taken at high tide, but not been too popular I had to help myself the best I could.

[103] 'While in Sydney I met a young lass and got married on 16 September [1903]' (French version, p. 82).

[104] Comment on the margin: 'Last news when she passed Newcastle.'

[105] Established in Bremen in 1857, the line started a regular subsidised service between Singapore and Kokopo in May 1893 (from 1886 to 1892 the New Guinea Company maintained a connection with Cooktown). The service was extended to Sydney in 1902. In 1904 the Singapore-Kokopo line ceased to operate and the Sydney-New Guinea service was extended to Hongkong and to Japanese ports, under the name of Austral-Japan Line. In April 1905 the Norddeutscher Lloyd agreed to maintain regular coastal service in the colony and offered favourable shipping terms to settlers who signed an exclusive five-year contract with it, thus forcing Burns, Philp and Co. to withdraw. The service between New Guinea and Singapore was re-opened in 1909.

The 'Muruna' was insured and the only loss I really had was the loss of Monrad and the abandon of all our prospects, I went to Sydney and I bought a secondhand boat a schooner of about 70 tons, which was christened 'Monantha' with Captain Strasburg[106] in charge, I used her to recruit and sometime take cargo of copra but it was only Greenwich for that work, I made a trip to Greenwich with her we stayed eight days, we had very bad luck on that trip, we took six weeks to make four hundred miles we had calm all that time we reached the equator, what we did at night we lost it in the day, and the heat was unbearable, at last a puff of wind came and we managed to reach Greenwich, our return back only took us four days, we had a good favourable wind and made good progress what a difference if we had only an engine what a lot of time it would have saved, from that time I came to the conclusion that the sailing vessel did not pay too much time wasted.

With the 'Monantha' I did not do much good Captain Strasburg recruited a few boys for me, and a trip to Greenwich and while in Buka he wrecked her after about eighteen months.

Captain Strasburg was stranded on an Island nearby where he was wrecked, the natives have been good to him so he did not suffer from them. I then had to charter the N.D.L. boat to pick him up and also on the insurance behalf, she was high and dry on the beach and the surveyor declared her a total wreck, this was in my favour because she was insured, only one man[107] thought he would be smart, he went with a shipful of bamboo and chartered the N.D.L. to pull her out, fortunately for me it was a failure, instead the failure cost the smart man a few hundred pounds, had he been able to save the vessel I would not have had the insurance and the result probably would be that I would have had to abandon the vessel to him to cover the cost. I was unfortunately insured against total loss, the man did not need to

[106] John Strasburg, a Swede by birth and a naturalised Australian since 1885. He had spent many years in New Guinea waters as the master of coastal schooners and was one of the founders of the New Britain Corporation, established in Sydney in 1907. He was engaged as a 'pilot for New Guinea waters' by the 1914 Australian Naval and Military Expeditionary Force and drafted the well-known Pidgin version of the Proclamation which marked the hoisting of the British flag in Rabaul (text in MacKenzie 1937: 76).

[107] Mouton is more explicit in the French version (p. 83), where 'one man' is replaced by 'the son of Mrs. Kolbe previously Mrs. Forsayth'.

do that and it only showed that he wanted to do as much harm as he could, I knew when he did not succeed the settlers were quite pleased about it. I received from the insurance eight hundred pounds and he lost three hundred pounds for the chartering alone plus the trouble of his labor to cut bamboo etc.

Now times have changed and the main thing for me was to be able to get labourers for my plantation, the other part of the trading business of taking copra etc. was done by the N.D.L. so I decided to buy a small boat if I could find one, at the time I could not go to Sydney and my friend Edward Lanser bought the 'Pactolus' of twenty tons with twin engines, she proved to be what I needed, she did a few trips as she was and did not do too bad, but to cope with the Administration requirement I had to make some alterations.

I employed chinese carpenters and had a cabin build on deck and a tank on the bow to carry the benzine,[108] this tank has been the ruin of the boat, the people who made the tank in Sydney did a very bad job, the tank leaked this tank was made to fit the bow of the boat and would be able to carry forty gallons of benzine, this would have been a great help, had it been so ordained she would have been the boat to fill my requirement, she had good speed and was very comfortable for a boat of that size.

The first day I put the benzine in the tank and were prepared for a trial the next morning, during the night I hear an explosion and there was the 'Pactolus' on fire, the cause of the fire was a boy smelling benzine lighted a match as soon as he did it he was blown in the air by force and was so badly burned that he died a few minutes after, unfortunately she was not insured the insurance had just expired and I forgot to renew it in due course, as she stood she cost me one thousand and six hundred pounds, the boat burned to rail and next morning at day break she disappeared in about ten fathom, we could see the engines on the bottom. J. C. M. Forsayth[109] who was always ready in a case

---

[108] German for petrol, the term was current on the Gazelle Peninsula during most of the 1920s and appeared in the *Rabaul Times* as late as 1927.

[109] Jonas Myndersee Coe Forsayth, son of Queen Emma from her first marriage, born in 1872, joined his mother in 1890 after some schooling in Sydney. He was left a portion of her interests when she sold out to Wahlen in 1910. He retired from New Guinea in 1913 and died in Sydney in 1941.

like this made me an offer for the engines, I was too disgusted with the whole thing that I was only too glad to let him have it, I think that it cost him a good bit to have those engines in good order, and I heard that he did not do any good with them it cost him all he got for it, and I quite believe it a secondhand engine which has been in fire was a thing hard to sell.

The 'Pactolus' originally's owner was a German who was the proprietor of the Surry Hotel at Bondi Junction I paid eight hundred pounds for her, the alteration made it a costly boat but she would have been worthwhile at the time and the expenses were justified. So there I am bad luck again with boat, the danger was when the boat burnt the blaze was so high the Mission shed full of timber was in great danger of setting on fire I think the only thing which saved the Mission was the land breeze blowing the flames out to sea.

It is wonderful through those bad luck I spend a fortune in bad luck with my boat, my plantation is the only thing which kept growing without much trouble, but then by putting the boat's bad luck against it, no doubt the plantation was responsible, fortunately the plantation kept her reputation and was able to bear the brunt. It was unfortunately a lack of discipline which caused the fire, strict instructions were given to the watchman not to light a fire or a match as there may be leakage in the tank and it would be dangerous to light a match this boy who was a Buka boy did just what he should not do, and the poor fellow pay with his life for it, and another drawback for me.

I must relate an incident which occurred while Monrad was in charge of the old 'Muruna', amongst the trading stations we had on the instigation of a German named Waffler we put him on Bougainville place called Ruburoi, he has an idea that at the back of the place there was a great possibility of a great district very rich in cocosnut palms and that it was only a matter of getting in touch with them, I and Monrad we did not know what to believe of it, at any rate without taking consideration of this castle in Spain, we gave him a chance, so we put him there with the necessary provisions and trade, and gave him a trial of six months, when we came at anchor to his place we found him very dishearted, his castle in Spain did not come through and he had to acknowledge that whoever told him pulled his leg, all he did was a patch of sweet potatoes and a bag or two of copra, it was while we were in Bougainville coast trying to recruit and at the same time seeing Waffler that we came across a canoe containing about six to eight rowers, we noticed that this canoe was making rather a wide circle and it was our principle to come in touch with the natives as much as possible, we made sign to come but of no avail, at last we had only one way of doing it, and we fire in front of the canoe, then they stood still and as we came close to the canoe we asked why they were afraid of us we had no intention to do them any harm, but in looking in the canoe we saw something covered in leafes, and on our request to see what it was, they lifted the covering and there was a body covered with blood, the natives told us that they were going to Numanuma to sell it. It is a strange thing that a part of Bougainville is not canibal but they are worse than canibal, it is a practice to entice the bush natives to come to the coast to barter with the coastal natives who are the guilty partie, the coastal native then manage to get some by himself knock him on the head and kill him then, the victim is brought to some neighbors who are canibal and are bought the same as they would a pig, having a ready market for human flesh, the coastal natives do their best to supply the market.

Sailing close to the coast we saw a lot of natives, who appeared to be bushmen, but no chance to go near them, they were always on the lookout, no sooner we made an attempt to go ashore they runaway, those were very wild natives and I do not think at that time any of them ever been with whitemen, but their fear was because they were hunted by the coast natives. Later when the whitemen managed to get in touch with them and the killing for canibalism were stopped, then recruits could be got from those parts of Bougainville.

The poor natives were rather handicapped even with the white recruiters, on one occasion the New Guinea Company Schooner 'Senta' did some funny recruiting, her crew would be dressed as police men and would lay in ambush and when the bush natives came down would surround them and take the best ones out of the bunch of course the recruits would be paid for just the same as if came willingly, in some cases such a method was quite justified, in some cases it was abused, that is it was justified when there was no other method to get in touch with the natives. With all the drawback in vessel line I managed to make a trip to Europe in 1908 at the time I had a good supply of labourers and the plantation was doing well, and the ice plant at Takubar with

Louri[110] in charge was going smoothly, I also relied upon Louri to keep an eye on the plantation which he did.

In May 1908 we boarded the 'Coblenz' at Sydney and sailed for Europe my wife and boy, the trip was the usual trip Captain Rondahl was on board too travelling with his wife Grace Coe and his boy Oscar, my boy was about four years then. Max.

After the usual mixed trip good and bad we arrived at Antwerp my mother was waiting for me, for twenty eight years we did not see one another, I was only fourteen when I left Belgium, but some way or another I recognised my mother at once, Rondahl stayed on board his destination was Stockholm, Sweden so he landed at Bremen.

We stayed in Belgium with my mother for about one month then we pay a visit to Germany we stayed one month in Hamburg, visited Berlin Kiel while we were there, only stayed in Berlin one week I forgot but I know that we spend a good deal of time in Germany, with my agent in Hamburg who was ready to supply me with the credit I wanted but did not take, we were quite allright unfortunately dragging children when [sentence incomplete]. Then we also stayed a good deal in Belgium with friends we stayed at Huy a small town on the River Meuse, while we were there a pilgrimage was arranged to visit Paris and spend one week in Paris, we were alltogether thirty members each paying so much, and at liberty to improve himself if wanted at his own extra expense, this was rather a good chance to see Paris, and I must say that we did see all what was to be seen, much better if we had gone by ourselves, because the trip was properly sheduled quarters were not the best, but we did not expect better for the money, the main thing is that we were not lonely, in our group there was Doctors, Lawyers and quite well-to-do peoples and their company was very agreeable, we had with us the daughter of our friend we were staying with Sapart, which I asked to go with us at my expense, she was quite thrilled

---

[110] Walter Louri, an engineer by trade. It appears that Mouton and Louri formed a public company to run the ice factory, for in the *Amtsblatt fuer das Schutzgebiet Deutsch- Neuguinea*, 1 February 1912, p. 33, there is an announcement that the company of Mouton and Louri had ceased to exist and that Louri started business under his own name. Takubar (a coastal locality) is not to be confused with Takabur which is situated inland from Kokopo.

to be able to come with us. I must say that the trip has been one of the best for so short a time, it was very agreeable.

From that trip to Paris then we went back to my mother for a while then it was time to think of thinking to make track home again, we did not visit London unfortunately, and we would not have visited Paris had we not have the opportunity we had, it is a shame we decided to go by train to Naples and go on board at Naples for the trip I used Cook, we left from Brussells for a trip to the Rhine and different excursions finishing with Naples, it was very nice but unfortunately every item of the trip is time-tabled and if one would like to spend a day some place during the trip it could not be done unless upsetting the whole arrangement, I quite agree there it would not be possible because generally there is a party as a rule large or small it is the same, we have to keep moving as per programme, for this reason Thomas Cook though very handy if one has plenty of money to spare it is better without Cook's Agency.

We stayed at Naples waiting for the N.D.L. Liner to pick us up, I think we had to wait more than one week, we were very pleased when the steamer arrived, from Naples we called at Ceylon Singapore Hong Kong, we stayed at Hongkong about one week at Hongkong Hotel, we had a rather pleasant time at Hongkong only it was very hot. The steamer we were waiting for was the 'Prinz Sigismund' going between Hong Kong Rabaul Sydney.

After returning from Europe, I became acquainted with a John Calder this was in 1910 he was a scotchman, he married an halfcast Samoan who had some properties in the Mortlock Islands,[111] it was in the beginning or the end of 1910 that Calder and Hoerler thought of starting a trading business, for this reason

[111] One of several 'lady companions' brought over by Queen Emma. She married Emma's accountant, Joseph Highley, and the couple was given Mortlock Islands as a wedding gift (Emma had 'bought' them in 1886 for £68 in trade goods). After her husband's death in 1894 Mrs Highley married John Calder; one of her daughters married a German medical officer, Dr Bruno Kroenig, and was under that name one of the respondents in the famous Mortlock Islands case heard in 1930 in the Central Court of the Territory of New Guinea before Mr Justice Phillips. Calder, before he died, founded the Bougainville Plantation Company with the intention of establishing a plantation on the island (French version, p. 85). His widow started a plantation there in 1912.

the three of us came to Sydney and I bought a vessel of about 96 tons capacity, with the understanding that each of the partners would pay his share in due time as progress improved, the vessel was called 'The Federal' as she was fitted with stern post capable of taking an engine shaft we agree to install an engine it was an Invincible engine of about 40 horse power, the boat got fitted and nearly completed when Calder became ill and had to go under an operation for kidney, before he went to the operation he made his Will, appointed me and G. Robertson as his executors, before the operation was performed before even the anaesthetic was administered he passed away, leaving his widow and me and Hoerler to fight the battle of the new enterprise.

So in 1911 I became Nationalized Australian so that we could fly the Australian flag, when the ship was properly fitted we gave a party on board before leaving, also a trial trip around the Harbour. Nelson & Robertson were then my agents and did all the necessary arrangements for the clearing of 'The Federal' our Captain was an old man Hoerler acted as mate and the engineer was a nephew of my wife Jim Scandlan, I left my wife in Sydney with my son and I left with 'The Federal' we left the Harbour very nicely the engine acted very well but that did not last long, it did not take long before one of the cylinder bearings become hot and burned so we were only using one cylinder, the vessel was not a good sailer, and the trip lasted a good while when we arrived at Giso British Solomons we were fortunate to have the engineer of the 'Matunga' to fix the bearing for us he melted the white metal and made a good job of it.

I was certainly very pleased that we could get the engine to work properly again, because as it was it would be a waste of fuel to use the engine, and only in case of emergency would I allow to do so and the Captain in that way was on my side, for one thing he did not believe in auxiliary ships, his moto give me sail or steam at any time, from Giso we made for Ontong Java this was the King goal of Hoerler it was his castle in Spain, according to his notion we were to do wonders, I had been dealing there before and therefore I had an old debt there to something like in the vicinity of five hundred pounds, the result of the death of King Weeler, his successor[112] did not look after our interests

[112] King Keaipea (Sarfert and Damm 1929: 9).

as established by Monrad some years ago, Hoerler had a wrong idea that he had a native wife from the place and he had also been trading for Mrs. Forsayth who was the only one who bought a piece of land from the natives, it was not much but it was a footing which was worth while to own.

Having given up Ontong Java after the disappearance of Monrad I was not aware of any change in the place, and Hoerler seemed to be very confident that things were for the best, he had nothing to lose all the loss were on my side, so after having look at the possibilities in all angles I pointed out to Hoerler, Mrs. Forsayth sold the bit of land she had on Ontong Java to Lever Bros. no doubt for a good price because it was worth it to Lever Bros. any one who thought to be able to do any business in opposition to Lever Bros. was mad, even the German who was supposed to wait for Hoerler did not wait and trade for Lever Bros. or rather for the Trader installed there by them.

The Ontong Java was knocked on the head there was nothing to be done there so I decided that it was a wild goose business, as we were not far from the coast of Bougainville we thought that we recruit some boys but I was very disappointed there during daytime we would get near enough the coast but at night the Captain instead of keeping along the coast he kept with full square sail out of the coast so at daybreak we found ourselve miles away from the coast, so it was no use to induce the Captain to keep the vessel in its proper direction what we win in the daytime it was lost at night through the pigheadedness of the Captain or rather I may say that the Captain was not too keen in coming in contact with the wild natives, but if he only knew he did not need to be scared of them at that time they were not so savages as I saw them years before but he was an old man and we could do nothing unless we mutiny, and that would have been a bad job, it was not worth risking, however after a day's trial I gave it up and we made for Kinigunan Kokopo being the Government Station, called then Herbertshoehe, strange to say we had a quick passage, it was like a horse making for his stable, on leaving Sydney it was understood that we would go to the Mortlocks and take delivery of Calder's Copra to dispose the best I could for her, but there we were disappointed on our arrival at Kinigunan the first news we got was that Mrs Calder sold the copra herself to someone else, I think it was to Hernsheim & Co. as she was quite justified to do so I had nothing to say about the matter, thought the copra was collected during Calder's lifetime it was not his property it was hers, had he been alife it would have been different, so the ship was of no much use to me to recruit it was too expensive she was too clumsy and slow she was good for what she was build for carry timber on the coast of New South Wales, she had all the appliances for that trade. Hoerler made one trip to Buka and brought a few boys and that all what the vessel ever made so I decided to send her back to Sydney and dispose of her, fortunately she did not stay long before she was sold to the Buka Trading Company starting a plantation at Bougainville Numanuma, I was glad of the transaction it was a little cash returning back to me but for all that it was a considerable loss for me just the same, with Calder out of action and the enterprise was too much for me I could not manage the Solomons, and I could not see any advantage in using more capital and by putting Hoerler in charge I am sure that I would have done the wrong thing. Hoerler went trading for somebody else I think he went to Ontong Java but he did not last very long after a few months I heard he was dead. This Company was formed under the name of Pacific Islands Company.[113]

In 1913 I had to have another vessel and I ordered the 'Takubar' from Holme Sr.[114] Mr. Barber Architect designed the vessel. I then made a short trip to Kinigunan I had then a German who managed my business and Plantation at Kinigunan and Rondahl's at Kabakaul. This man had a very good name having managed the business part for the New Guinea Company, and

---

[113] Correct in substance but not in detail. The Buka Trading Company, established in Sydney in October 1912, was one of several companies formed by Lever's Pacific Plantations Ltd to work their holdings in the south-west Pacific. The connection between Lever Brothers and the Pacific Islands Company dates from the turn of the century when William Lever decided that his crushing mills in Sydney should be supplied from their own copra plantations. In 1901 he invested in J. T. Arundel's Pacific Islands Company with its extensive plantation and mining interests. In 1902 the company was wound up and its phosphate mining interests were taken over by the Pacific Phosphate Company, of Nauru and Ocean Island fame, while the plantation interests were assigned to Lever's Pacific Plantations Ltd. Lever started expanding into the Solomons in 1905 and had a financial interest in the already mentioned New Britain Corporation (fn. 97). For more information on the Lever Brothers' empire see Wilson 1954.

[114] Comment on the margin: 'Berry Bay'.

he proved a good competent accountant but rather extravagant in ordering goods supply, he never could forget that we were not like the New Guinea Company who was a powerful concern, six months after he took the management I made a short trip to see how thing were going on, the 'Harriet Alice' was doing a little recruiting and Mueller complained about the Captain who did not prove very satisfactory he turned out a drunker, well trouble again, I also found out that the overseer of the plantation a German the boys complained to me that he was very cruel to the boys, of which I informed Mueller that the overseer was doing very cruel things and was hated by the boys, and that he better see to it if he did not want trouble later, but he poo-hoohed and said that the boys did not tell the truth, that the overseer was a very good man he made the boys work well, and that the boys are only complaining because he made them do their work, this was quite possible but the complaints made to me did not agree with his statement, this overseer was a young man and seemed to understand his work.

However, not very long after my return to Sydney I received the news that this Overseer had committed suicide by taking arsenic, it appear that he was found out and that the German authorities were going to deal with the matter so he did not like to face the music. I may state here that between this period I got divorced and married again, this rather private matter do not need to be mentioned.

On the end of July 1914 me and my wife we left by the 'Koblenz' for Rabaul, arrived at Rabaul a couple of days before the declaration of the great war, while on board yet on hearing of the assasination of the Archduke the german passengers said we will have war and they seemed very joyful about it, amongst the passengers Mr. Mark Foy was one of them.

As soon as the news arrived the 'Koblenz' left Rabaul with Mark Foy on board, I understand that he was landed in the Carolines where he managed to hire a boat and got out to friendly national, I am not acquainted of what happen to him only by hearsay, I only met him in Sydney some years after, but did not converse with him as he was in hurry he had his son with him I think. Well here we are the war is declared and we are in Germany territory and to my surprise in a few days all the police boys received military uniforms and the number of police boys were greatly augmented, it looked to me that the Germans had expected that war would come soon and no doubt by the preparations made it was not a surprise to them,[115] and they boasted in a few days we will be in Paris that is at the start, so they thought that they would walk through Belgium and from there to Paris, they were quite disappointed when it lasted longer than they expected.

My manager Mueller was a German and was held responsible for us, all the German planters and civilians became soldiers and had to be under military control, of course they knew what was going on through the wireless but we did not know and the Germans did not enlighten us they kept all the news to themselves. We were informed that we were not at liberty to leave Kabakaul and only at liberty to visit Kinigunan with K. B. Mueller, this kept going until the first Australian Navy came to Rabaul they landed at Kokopo made a mess of the Post Office then went back and disappeared altogether, we were ordered to leave Kabakaul and go to Kulon a Property of Rondahl a few miles along the coast, with instruction not to leave the place we were guarded by a couple of civilians dressed in khaki uniforms.

We did not know what to make out of this, but by what the guards say and the vigil they were doing it was plain that they expected something, and sure enough about a week after the first visit the 'Australia' and the 'Brisbane' arrived and a couple of days later the first convoy with soldiers arrived, they landed some of them at Kabakaul and proceeded to Bitapaka the wireless station on the road they were met by the police and all the German force available, and in the action a few men were killed and wounded one of them Dr. Pockley, a German Ritter, and a few soldiers, the Germans were ambushed along the road,[116]

---

[115] Mouton was right in his assumption, up to a point. Late in 1913 the administration toyed with the idea of introducing compulsory 'police service' for men between the age of sixteen and thirty not in plantation employment. An ordinance to that effect was prepared (the earliest draft referred to 'military service' but this was later changed to 'police service', for fear of international repercussions) but the idea was shelved in favour of a vigorous recruiting drive coupled with better conditions of service. The draft budget for 1915 authorised an increase in the police force from about 650 to 1000, and some 120 additional men were recruited by August 1914 (CAO, AA 63/83, Box 205, Item A 10).

[116] The other way around. The Germans had prepared an ambush along the Bitapaka road but it failed, because of the poor performance of the native soldiers (Mackenzie 1937: 55-61). The book also discusses looting by Australian troops referred to by Mouton in the same paragraph.

the Australian force took Bitapaka in no time but not before the Germans blowed out the Wireless, this however was reconstructed in a few days. Now we were under the Australian military controle, and the next day after the taking of Bitapaka we were informed to appear at Kokopo before the military commandant, our Manager Mueller was a prisoner at the time on board one of the ships, and we decided to leave Kulon and live at Takubar my plantation, Mueller did not stay long a prisoner, the next day he was free, Rondahl went back to Kakabaul and we stayed at Takubar, during the landing the force looted Rondahl's Store at Kakabaul but the drink stuff was the main loot, at my place at Kinigunan where I had my store and Takubar they did not loot one of my Boys told the soldiers that I was not a German, so they let my belongings alone.

While this was going on my boat the 'Harriet Alice' was prisoner in Kavieng during the German time after the declaration, and the Captain who was a bad egg made himself notorious by helping himself in the German store with the liquor he could get and make a beast of himself and when he arrived he did not last long I had to get rid of him. Times were not too bright we had a drought and food for the labourers was very scarce, my Manager unfortunately was not too good and it was fortunate for me that I arrived in time, my first move being to save all the planted food by cleaning the whole lot of weed, which was taking the controle of the field, this I think saved the situation, I started that as soon I arrived from Sydney before the landing of the troop ship.

The country being under the Military Administration the routine returned to the usual, only food became scarce and it was with great relief that we saw the 'Moresby' arrive with some rice, I only wanted rice for my boys but I had to take a certain quantity of preserve meat as well to obtain rice from Burns Philp & Co. Ltd.

From that time on I and Rondahl came to the conclusion that Mueller was a bad Manager[117] and we agree to get rid of him, Rondahl did not like the idea at first but I told him that he could have him if he wanted that I would give him notice, so he did

---

[117] Comment on the margin: 'Was only partner with Rondahl some years before in business not in plantation.'

also and we were glad to get rid of him, we could not forget that he was our gaoler for a time. I managed my plantation after that, then while I was managing I received a letter from a Belgian named Vancant who asked for the job, it was in the beginning of 1915 I wanted to go to Sydney to see about the ship in the way of construction so I engaged this man who arrived by the next steamer, I did not know him but before I left I had a pretty good idea that he would not be the man, however I gave him instruction to get rid of the 'Harriet Alice' which he did by selling the ship for six hundred pounds on credit to the Japanese Komine,[118] while I was at Takubar one named Leslie pay me visit then he was Manager of a Firm at Samarai and by his talk I thought that he must be a good man, but this gentleman will be referred to later.

In the beginning of 1915 the 'Matunga' arrived and I decided to leave by her she came to my place to take a load of copra then we went on board, I left Vancant Manager of my plantation but with uneasiness, the next mail gave me bad news I heard that he was half mad and was doing lot of foolishness, so while I was in Sydney Leslie came to see me and asked me for the position of manager, not knowing better I jumped on the good fortune which give me a good man I thought, because I thought being manager of the British Company at Samarai he would be the man I wanted, so I accepted his offer, so he went to Rabaul and with my instruction got Vancant out of the way and took his place. On the completion of my new ship 'Takubar' I send her to Rabaul Captain Fendick being master it must have been in May 1915 or perhaps a little earlier but I know it was a little before my boy was born and he was born on the 31st of May, 1915. Leopold.

---

[118] Captain Isokide Komine, the leader of the Japanese community in Rabaul, settled in New Guinea in 1902, started a shipyard in 1907 and brought out the first Japanese tradesmen to settle in the colony in 1910 (not to mention four ladies of easy virtue who had arrived some five years earlier). He had extensive plantation interests on Manus and was said to be worth £70,000 in 1919. Note marginal comment: 'Komini [sic] was boat builder, rogue. Fled Rabaul.' This is a reference to his 'escape' to Japan, late in 1913, after Hernsheim and Co. had applied for an order for his arrest because he would not pay his debts. After his return Komine was advanced money by the Australian military administration 'on account of his financial embarrassment' (CAO, CP 661/15, folder 4).

Leslie then wrote to me that Captain Fendick may not suit however I went back to Rabaul to see how thing were going on my wife stayed in Sydney, as soon as I arrived at Rabaul I made a trip to Greenwich, there I found the copra very dry and of poor quality, also they had the drought and things looked very bad, and I come to the decision that I would have to give up Greenwich which was under the Japanese rule, at the best time the most it gave was seventy tons of copra and subject to drought and at the time there was no prospect so I gave it up with a loss of a couple thousand pounds, would be more if I kept going beside the distance was 400 miles from my place too far for the result, while Monrad was alive he was very interested in the Island because his Girl and children were there and during his time there never was such a bad time as it was now, but the native yarn point out that there has been droughts before which caused a lot of damages to human lives, so this is my last trip to Greenwich, and another failure.

I ordered the 'Takubar' before the war and in my prospect Greenwich was an asset as a working proposition for her.

Having visited Greenwich and having a good Manager as I thought it would be after I went with him showing how to work the plantation, which of course he knew better than I did, I left Kinigunan again, I must explain here that Takubar was the dwelling where the Overseer lived and Louri before, Kinigunan is the main dwelling but owing to the change made to have a Manager for Kabakaul and Kinigunan the dwelling at Kinigunan remained neglected during the Management of the German Manager Mueller, so when mentioning Kinigunan in this stage is because it is occupied again.

I stayed in Sydney for about ten months then I went back to Kinigunan during my absence Leslie had to get rid of Captain Fendick and when I arrived he had a new man named Hawker who was only a sailor and had no Master certificate, I thought that it was a bad plan to do that he had the permit to sail the vessel allright but it was not the thing according to my way of thinking and it turned out wrong later on.

This man kept the 'Takubar' like a Man-of-war boat and the vessel looked beautiful she was well painted and kept clean, and while I was there this Hawker got married, he took his wife with him on the 'Takubar'. He was instructed to recruit boys for the plantation, all the recruiting he did was to have a good honeymoon at my expense, he returned with only one boy which cost me over £100 because I had to send him back etc. I also noticed that he had ordered petrol and signed for it but no record to be seen, I came to the conclusion that he did not do straight dealing and that he was in understanding with the Chinamen and Japanese, fortunately for me I came back in time and saw at once that he was the wrong man, I found out that the sails were rotten, owing to neglecting to use them and to put them to dry, this man was running the vessel on petrol, never used the sail, the way it was going on was simply ruinous still my Manager did not see it or did not want to see it, having inspected the ship and discovering the deceiving part of the man in charge I dismissed him, and ordered the boat to put at anchore at Rabaul with a few boys as caretakers, this man threaten me that he would go for damage, I told him that the damage was on my side if he wanted to go on he must know that all I had to do was to show the state of the sails, it would be enough for any seaman to understand. That settled the matter he knew that I had him there.

The 'Takubar' was put to anchore at Rabaul for a time then I engaged a man who had some experience, but before he left for a trip he got on the booze and I did not think it was safe to let him go ahead. Then I got a Swede from Sydney who took charge he did not do too bad but it turned out rather expensive so the vessel did not pay and it turned out to be a white Elephant to me, however I had to keep the ship going, I then engaged a former captain send him to recruit with an help for recruiting the result was that he did not help the recruiter and the vessel returned empty so by the report I received from the recruiter this Captain was of no use, then I came to the conclusion if I could charter her or let her it would be better for me than lose money as I did, so after failing with the Government I chartered the ship to the German New Guinea Company just for the keeping of the ship provided they kept me with the labourers required, this turned out good for me and one of the Captains who had been with me now was in charge I got the first recruits as stipulated and after three trips he wrecked the 'Takubar' on the South coast of New Britain,[119] she was insured for two thousand pounds

[119] Comment on the margin: 'About 1916 or 1917 wrecked'.

she cost me three thousand but in a way she had been a white Elephant to me so far, and it was the best thing it could have happen.

After having inspected my plantation I saw that the plantation was neglected and that those parts to be seen by the public were kept clean and my manager when I told him that the plantation was very much neglected told me that he could not see how it could be cleaned better, of course I must give him credit he did what he thought was right, but after I took the working of the plantation for a couple of weeks he saw the difference, so I came to the conclusion after seeing that he did not even kept the books though he ordered very expensive set of books they were not used, I then gave him notice we parted good friends but he was useless so I managed the plantation again myself that was in the later end of 1919 then my wife mentioned a friend of hers who may likely be a good man for me, I did not think so at first but after all I will give it a trial, so this man came and I thought he was what I wanted and so he was until later.

At the end of 1919 I made up my mind to make a trip to Europe to see my mother in Belgium, we were three myself my wife my child and a nurse, there is nothing special with a trip to Europe we stayed in London, Paris, Brussels and Namur most of the time as it was not far from where my mother lived, unfortunately we arrived just after the war and we found the hotels and tourist accommodation very bad, the only advantage we had was that we were able to see the damage done by the war which was worth the inconvenience of the accommodation.

We stayed ten months, while I was away my manager wrote to me that the authorities were making trouble regarding my nationality, on the ground that I had been naturalized a German subject, no doubt it would have been acceptable in a point of view of asset for the Expropriation Board, unfortunately for them and fortunately for me I was naturalized in Australia in 1911, when this was proved by my Solicitor in Sydney that ended the case, however, I thought that it was time to make my way back and see for myself, so we returned to Sydney in 1920.

Through the advice of my friend I applied for the new naturalization the Empire Naturalization which I was granted, then I went to my plantation, at the time my manager was due for a holiday so I managed the plantation and he went to Sydney with his wife and child.

I had made arrangements that he should come back at first I had not much time to see what had been done, and it could only be ascertained by time and working the plantation, the reports given to me were to the good and I thought that I did not make a mistake in having him back I even increased his salary.

No sooner I had the plantation under my controle I was able to find that my manager was not what I thought he was, the plantation was very much neglected and I found out that the reports were only made according to what their eyes were able to see, after about one week's work I found out that even the nuts were not collected and were left to sprout in the plantation because the plantation was so dirty that the nuts could not be seen, what a good time the labourers must have had, it took me six months hard work to get the plantation in order again, during this manager's controle I must have lost nearly one hundred tons of copra at the price of copra at the time my loss was about £2,500, it was unfortunate for him that he was too fond of society and the two cannot go together the plantation was left in charge of a Guam overseer who on his part should have known better, having been under me for over several years.

So it was a surprise to me as well as my manager when I had to cancel any future engagement and broke the agreement, of course the usual threat of ligitation occurred but it did not come to anything because facts were too strong against him so he stayed in Sydney and it was the last with the only exception that I met him occasionally in Sydney but with the old hatchet buried.

I tried my son but he was too young and too weak as a boss, I found out that he was the tool for other people's benefit, and too fond of outing so after I gave him two trials each of six months, I found out that the last six months were worse than the first ones so I had against my heart to give it up, it was between the plantation being ruined and business neglected had I let it go further under my son's management.

So against all my best wishes for my son to take charge of the plantation I had to engage another manager I knew Mr. Hooger-werff Hollander so I made arrangement with him, my son was then under him, but my son felt rather humiliated, and both did not agree very well he could not see that it was his own fault that it was so, but what is the use one cannot teach sense in fools, we have also to take in consideration that there are people about, who only relish through jealousie or envie to put their little poison dart into the weakbrained.

Well my son went and tried his luck mining, but like the rest through his foolishness failed by trusting too much to others and by not acting on his own counsel.

I must say that under Mr. Hoogerwerff I had to stay at the plantation a good while but not on account of the plantation because I found out that Mr. Hoogerwerff after knowing the proper way of working did not need looking after and having put his heart in it there was no cause for me to interfere, so I could put all my time in building works.

In the later end of 1929 I had an offer to come in partnership with the printing of 'Rabaul Times' against warning I accepted, and signed the contract trusting the proposer, I was bound for twenty one years or I must get out at the cost of nine thousand and all the deceased Hamilton's[120] debts had to be paid, meanwhile the proposer or my partner[121] started Picture show[122] and restaurant, the upkeep of which I had to pay after spending about seven thousand pounds in clearing picture show and restaurant I came to the conclusion to make a stop, meanwhile my partner had a proposition from a London Syndicate to buy plantations, and I offered mine for Eighty five thousand pounds cash no terms, the option money I did not ask for, which I should have done, he being my partner in the 'Rabaul Times' paper I thought that I would leave him have the benefit of it, first option failed then I give a second option of three months, after the second option then I was approached by the Catholic Mission, to my surprise because Bishop Couppé[123] told me that the Mission would not

[120] Harry William Hamilton, arrived in New Guinea in 1915, became Government Printer soon after and held the position until it was abolished in 1923. He started the *Rabaul Times* as a weekly in April 1924, with the motto: 'Our journal stands for progress'. He died in October 1927 and the paper was taken over from his widow in January 1929 by St James Enterprises, owned by Francis Geraghty, formerly of W. R. Carpenter and Co. Ltd. Between 1925-27 the paper was edited by Gordon Thomas (see f.n. 124).

[121] Comment on the margin: 'Garrity [i.e. Geraghty] now dead was partner with Rabaul Times.'

[122] The St James Pictures, later called the Regent.

[123] Comment on the margin: 'Bishop Couppé had told me that he couldnt buy it years before He was dead then Bishop Vester[s] was in charge Hollander.'

147

buy my plantation, and the Mission was also surprised that the late Bishop could say such a thing, then I agreed with the Mission that after the option was expired that I would sell the Plantation to the Mission, on the date of the option expiring a Lady asked for another option in the name of a London Syndicate just for a few days, I turned her down and accepted the Mission offer which was closed with a deposit of twenty thousand pounds, that settled the London business.

After having settled this option then I came to the conclusion that I must ask my partner to resign in the 'Rabaul Times' concern which he did owing to the fact that he was unable to pay his share in the business. Having settled the partnership and the Mission transaction, I made use of my option to pay nine thousand pounds to get clear of the agreement binding me to twenty one years, to the unwillingness of the parties concerned, this business was at last terminated at the cost of sixteen thousands pounds in all,[124] and now I am the owner of the 'Rabaul Times'. So far this paper do not give me an income but it keep itself going and having Mr Hoogerwerff as manager cause me no worry and the institution give work to some people at Rabaul, as well as keeping the Rabaul residents informed of the news of the world, I think by so doing I have kept going a concern which benefit the Territory, and if there is nothing else in a way of remuneration I have at least given some pleasure to the territory residents, by enabling them to have the 'Rabaul Times' kept going which would have perished under the former owner. Now after my hard labour and hard time of the past I have at least the benefit of my hardship.

[124] Comment on the margin: 'With picture show and all now . . . £3,500' (one word illegible). The deal was finalised in January 1931 when Mouton established the Rabaul Printing Works. In June 1933 the editorship of the *Rabaul Times* was taken over again by Edward Llewellyn Gordon Thomas, usually known as Gordon Thomas, who started his New Guinea days in 1911 as a Methodist mission printer, worked as an oil driller and ran a plantation on Bougainville. Thomas was one of the few civilians to survive the Japanese occupation of Rabaul—most of the 300 civilian prisoners drowned in May 1942 when the ship which was taking them to Japan, the *Montevideo Maru*, was sunk by an allied torpedo.

References

Adressbuch fuer Deutsch-Neuguinea, Samoa, Kiautschou.
1912. Berlin.

Australia, British Administration—(Late) German
New Guinea. 1916. *Statistics Relating to Commerce,
Native Tax, Population, Live Stock and Agriculture, etc.
in Connexion with the Late German New Guinea Possessions.* Melbourne.

Australia, Interstate Commission. 1918. *Report on
the South Pacific Trade.* Melbourne.

Australia, Royal Commission on Late German
New Guinea. 1920. *Interim and Final Reports.* Melbourne.

Australian Naval Station. 1881. *Reporting Proceedings in the Solomons, New Britain, New Guinea, etc.:
Deputy-Commissioner Romilly to the High Commissioner, Brisbane, August 6th 1881.*

Barrett, C. 1954. *Isles of the Sun.* Melbourne.

Bassett, M. 1969. *Letters from New Guinea, 1921.*
Melbourne.

Battistessa, F. 1934. 'Dall' Incubo di Liki-Liki alla
Speranza di New Italy', *Vade Mecum (Trade &
Social Guide for Italians in Australia)*: 82-92.

Baudouin, A. 1885. *L'Aventure de Port-Breton et la
Colonie Libre dite Nouvelle-France.* Paris.

Becke, L. 1899. 'The South Sea Bubble of Charles
du Breil', in *Ridan the Devil and Other Stories.*
London: 233-43.

Bley, B. 1924. *Die Herz-Jesu-Mission in der Suedsee.*
Hiltrup.

Blum, H. 1900. *Neu-Guinea und der Bismarck-Archipel*. Berlin.

Boegerhausen, G. n.d. 'Das Paradies der Suedsee'. MS in possession of Mrs D. K. Groves, Hawthorn, Victoria. Microfilm copy PMB 613, Pacific Manuscripts Bureau.

Bougainville, L. A. 1772. *A Voyage Round the World*. London, translated from French by J. R. Forster.

Brown, G. 1908. *George Brown, D. D. Pioneer—Missionary and Explorer: An Autobiography*. London.

Capell, A. 1967. 'A Lost Tribe in New Ireland', *Mankind*, **6** (10): 499-509.

Cayley-Webster, H. 1898. *Through New Guinea and the Cannibal Countries*. London.

Collinbride, G. 1923. 'Colonization by Prospectus', *Forum*, **1** (24): 14.

'Colonization in the South Seas'. 1880-81. *Proceedings of the Royal Geographical Society*, **2** (new series): 369-70 and **3**: 47.

La Colonie Libre de Port-Breton: Nouvelle France en Océanie. 1879. Marseilles.

La Colonie Libre de Port-Breton: Nouvelle France (Océanie): Exposé Sommaire. 1882. Marseilles.

Costantini, A. 1907. *Theoretisch-praktischer Lehrgang der Neu-Pommern Sprache*. Berlin.

Danks, B. 1887. 'On the Shell Money of New Britain', *Journal of the Anthropological Institute of Great Britain and Ireland*, **17**: 305-17.

Danks, B. 1933. *In Wild New Britain: the Story of Benjamin Danks, Pioneer Missionary, from his Diary*. Ed. W. Deane. Sydney.

Danks, B. 1934. 'A French Tragedy of the South Seas', *Life* (Melbourne), 15 January: 26-27, 85.

Daudet, A. 1890. *Port-Tarascon*. Paris.

Denham, J. T. n.d. Notes on New Guinea and the Solomons, 1915-1923. Typescript, Mitchell Library.

Deutscher Kolonial-Kalender Und Statistisches Handbuch Fuer Das Jahr 1914. 1914. Berlin.

Deutsches Kolonial-Lexikon. 1920. Leipzig, 3 vols.

Dupeyrat, A. 1935. *Papouasie: Histoire de la Mission (1885-1935)*. Issoudun.

Eggleston, F. W. ed. 1928. *The Australian Mandate for New Guinea*. Melbourne.

Eilers, A. 1934. *Inseln um Ponape*. Hamburg (Ergebnisse der Suedsee-Expedition, 1908-1910, II, Ethnographie: B: Mikronesien, Band 8).

Emory, K. P. 1965. *Kapingamarangi*. Honolulu.

Encyclopaedia of Papua and New Guinea. 1972. Melbourne, 3 vols.

Epstein, T. S. 1968. *Capitalism, Primitive and Modern: Some Aspects of Tolai Economic Growth.* Canberra.

'Expedition Nach Neu—Meckenburg Sued'. 1905. *Deutsche Kolonialzeitung*, **22**: 195-96.

Festetics de Tolna, R. 1904. *Vers l'Ecueil de Minicoy.* Paris.

Finsch, O. 1880. 'Ein Brief aus Matupi'. *Zeitschrift fuer Ethnologie*, **12**: 402-04.

Finsch, O. 1882. 'Briefe aus Neu—Britannien' *Zeitschrift der Gesellschaft fuer Erdkunde*, **16**: 293-305.

Finsch, O. 1887. 'Ueber die Naturprodukte der Westlichen Suedsee, besonders der deutschen Schutzgebiete', *Deutsche Kolonialzeitung*, **4**: 519-30, 543-51, 593-96.

Finsch, O. 1888. *Samoafahrten.* Leipzig.

Firth, S. 1972. 'The New Guinea Company, 1885-1899: a Case of Unprofitable Imperialism', *Historical Studies*, **15** (59): 361-77.

German New Guinea. 1901-1914. *Annual Reports.*

De Groote, P. 1880. *Nouvelle-France: Colonie Libre de Port-Breton (Océanie).* Paris.

Groves, W. C. 1925. 'Peter the Island King.' MS in the possession of Mrs D. K. Groves, Hawthorn, Victoria. Microfilm copy PMB 612, Pacific Manuscripts Bureau.

Hahl, A. 1897. 'Ueber die Rechtsanschauungen der Eingeborenen eines Theiles der Blanchebucht und des Innern der Gazellehalbinsel', *Nachrichten ueber Kaiser Wilhelmsland*, **13**: 68-85.

Hahl, A. 1907. 'Das Mittlere Neumecklenburg' *Globus*, **91** (20): 310-16.

Hahl, A. 1936. *Deutsch-Neuguinea.* Berlin.

Hassert, K. 1903. *Die neuen deutschen Erwerburgen in der Suedsee.* Leipzig.

Healy, A. M. 1965. 'Ophir to Bulolo: the History of the Gold Search in New Guinea', *Historical Studies*, **12** (45): 105-18.

Henderson, W. O. 1962. *Studies in German Colonial History.* London.

Hueskes, J. ed. 1932. *Pioniere der Suedsee.* Hiltrup.

Jouët, V. 1887. *La Societé des Missionnaires du Sacré Coeur dans les Vicariats Apostoliques de la Mélanésie et de la Micronésie.* Issoudun.

Kleintitschen, A. 1906. *Die Kuestenbewohner der Gazellehalbinsel.* Hiltrup.

Kraemer, A. 1927. *Palau.* Hamburg (Ergebnisse der Suedsee-Expedition 1908-1910, II, Ethnographie: B: Mikronesien, Band 3).

Kraemer-Bannow, E. 1909 *Bei kunstsinnigen Kannibalen der Suedsee: Wanderungen auf Neu-Mecklenburg, 1908-1909.* Berlin.

Laracy, H. 1973. *The Italians in New Zealand, and other Studies.* Auckland.

'Lask Link With de Rays Horror'. 1956. *Pacific Islands Monthly*, **26** (7): 127.

Leach, H. N. 1916. 'Marquis de Rays' Expedition'. *Rabaul Record*, 1 May: 9-10.

Leidecker, C. 1916. *Im Lande des Paradiesvogels.* Leipzig.

Leutwein, P. ed. n.d. *Dreissig Jahre deutsche Kolonialpolitik.* Berlin.

Lyng, J. 1916. 'German New Guinea', *Rabaul Record*, 1 July: 10-12; 1 August: 6-9; 1 September: 8-11; 1 October: 11-14; 1 November: 4-7.

Lyng, J. 1919. *Our New Possession (Late German New Guinea).* Melbourne.

Lucas-Dubreton, J. 1929. *L'Eden du Pacifique.* Paris.

Mackellar, C. D. 1912. *Scented Isles and Coral Gardens.* London.

Mackenzie, S. S. 1937. *The Australians at Rabaul.* Sydney.

'A Marquis de Rays Link Broken'. 1956. *Pacific Islands Monthly*, **26** (2): 129.

Mead, M. 1960. 'The Weaver of the Border', in J. B. Casagrande, ed. *In the Company of Man.* New York: 176-210.

Mensch, F. and Hellman, J. 1912. *Von der Heydt's Kolonial-Handbuch.* Berlin.

Michener, J. A. and Grove Day, A. 1957. 'Charles I, Emperor of Oceania', in *Rascals in Paradise.* London: 51-79.

Niau, J. H. 1936. *The Phantom Paradise.* Sydney.

Niau, M. H. 1930. *Souvenir d'une Parisienne aux Antipodes.* Sydney.

Nevermann, H. 1934. *Admiralitaets-Inseln.* Hamburg. (Ergebnisse der Suedsee-Expedition 1908-1910, II, Ethnographie: A: Melanesien, Band 3).

New Guinea Company. 1887-1896. *Annual Reports.*

Overell, L. A. 1923. *A Woman's Impression of German New Guinea.* London.

Parkinson, R. 1887. *Im Bismarck-Archipel.* Leipzig.

Parkinson, R. 1898. 'Nachtraege zur Ethnographie der Ontong-Java-Inseln', *Internationales Archiv fuer Ethnographie*, **11**: 194-209.

Parkinson, R. 1907. *Dreissig Jahre in der Suedsee.* Stuttgart.

Pitcairn, W. D. 1891. *Two Years Among the Savages of New Guinea*. London.

Port Breton: Colonia Libre En Océania. 1881. Madrid.

Poulain, J. 1883. *Le Rocher de Port-Breton*. Nantes.

Powell, W. 1884. *Wanderings in a Wild Country*. London.

Preuss, P. 1916. 'Wirtschaffliche Werte in den deutscher Suedseekolonien', *Tropenpflanzer*, **19** (10): 539-61.

Le Procès du Marquis de Rays: une Tentative de la Colonie Chrétienne devant la Justice Française. 1884. Marseilles.

Pullen-Burry, B. 1908. *In a German Colony*. London.

Radi, H. 1971. 'New Guinea under Mandate 1921-41' in W. J. Hudson, ed. *Australia and Papua and New Guinea*. Sydney: 74-137.

Reche, O. 1954. *Nova Britannia*. Hamburg (Ergebnisse der Suedsee-Expedition 1908-1910, II, Ethnographie: A: Melanesien, Band 4).

Reed, S. W. 1943. *The Making of Modern New Guinea*. Philadelphia.

Rin, E. da n.d. 'Italiani in Australia: la Saga di "Nuova Italia".' TS, Italian Embassy, Canberra.

Robson, R. W. 1965. *Queen Emma*. Sydney.

Romilly, H. H. 1887. *The Western Pacific and New Guinea*. London.

Rowley, C. D. 1958. *The Australians in German New Guinea 1914-1921*. Melbourne.

Sack, P. G. 1971. Traditional Land Tenure and Early European Land Acquisitions: The Clash Between Primitive and Western Law in New Guinea. Ph.D. thesis, Australian National University.

Sack, P. G. 1973. *Land Between Two Laws: Early European Land Acquisitions in New Guinea*. Canberra.

Salisbury, R. F. 1962. 'Early Stages of Economic Development in New Guinea', *Journal of the Polynesian Society*, **71**: 328-39.

Salisbury, R. F. 1967. 'Pidgin's Respectable Past', *New Guinea*, **2** (2): 44-48.

Salisbury, R. F. 1970. *Vunamami: Economic Transformation in a Traditional Society*. Berkeley.

Sapper, K. 1910. *Beitraege zur Landeskunde von Neu-Mecklenburg und seiner Nachbarinseln*. Berlin (Mitteilungen aus den deutschen Schutzgebieten, Ergaenzungsheft No. 3).

Sapper, K. 1915. 'Die deutschen Suedseebesitzungen', *Geographische Zeitschrift*, **21**: 624-45.

Sarfert, E. and Damm, H. 1929. *Luangiua—und Nukumanu*, Hamburg (Ergebnisse der Suedsee-

Expedition 1908-1910, II, Ethnographie: B: Mikronesien, Band 12).

Sceusa, F. 1881. *La Spedizione del Marchese di Rays e le Sue Victime*. Sydney.

Schlaginhaufen, O. 1908. 'Streifzuege in New-Mecklenburg und Fahrten nach benachbarten Inselgruppen', *Zeitschrift fuer Ethnologie*, **40**: 952-57.

Scholefield, G. H. 1919. *The Pacific: Its Past and Future*. London.

Schnee, H. 1904. *Bilder aus der Suedsee*. Berlin.

'Spotlight on the Mortlocks and Tasmans', 1968. *Pacific Islands Monthly*, **39** (2): 85-87.

Stephan, E. 1905. 'Ein modernes Kolonialabenteuer' *Globus*, **88**: 325-31, 349-53.

Stephan, E. and Graebner, F. 1907. *Neu Mecklenburg*. Berlin.

Tappenbeck, E. 1900. 'Samoamuenzen', *Deutsche Kolonialzeitung*, **13**: 534-35.

Townsend, G. L. W. 1968. *District Officer*. Sydney.

Truppel, G. 1880. 'Die Aussichten im Bismarck-Archipel' *Deutsche Kolonialzeitung*, **1** (new series): 287-90.

Tudor, J. 1949. 'The Marquis Provided the Millstone', *Pacific Islands Monthly*, **21** (7): 43-44.

De Valamont, P. 1889. *La Verité sur la Colonie de Port-Breton et sur le Marquis de Rays*. Nîmes (not sighted).

Valentine, C. A. 1963. An Introduction to the History of Changing Ways of Life on the Island of New Britain. Ph.D. thesis, University of Pennsylvania.

Wawn, W. T. 1893. *The South Sea Islanders and the Queensland Labour Trade*. London.

Wichman, A. 1909. *Nova Guinea*, vol. 1, Leiden.

Wichman, A. 1910. *Nova Guinea*, vol. 2, pt. 2. Leiden.

Wilson, C. 1954. *The History of Unilever*. London, 2 vols.

Wurm, S.A. 1966. 'Pidgin—a National Language', *New Guinea*, **1** (6): 49-54.

INDEX

Aden, *40*
Adler, *90*
Admiralty Islands, *22*, *25*, *117-18*, *119, 121, 142*
adultery, *103-4*
akai, *110*
aku, *108*
Alim Island, *48n.*
Antverps, *8*, *134*
Arimoa Island, *46-7*
Arnoldi, Captain von, *113n.*
Armand family, *80n.*
Arundel, T. J., *138n.*
Australia, *140*
Austral-Japan Line, *129n.*
L'Aventure de Port-Breton, *18*
Australian Naval and Military Expeditionary Force, *130n.*, *140-1*

Bahar, 'Chief', *94n.*
Baie Française, *52n.*
Baining Mountains, *122*
Balgai, *25*
bananas, *105-6*
Barcelona, *8*, *38*, *67n.*, *74n.*
Barcelona, *67n.*
Barry, N. C., *81n.*
Baudouin, A.: *12*, *18-19*, *63*, *65;*
return to France, *66n.*

155

Stalio, Agostino, *113n.*
Strasburg, Captain, *130*
Strella, 117
Suez, *40*
Sumatra, *46*
sweet potato, *124n.*
Sydney, *2, 123, 126-7, 136, 139*

Tabakur, *134n*
Tabar, *see* Gardner Islands
Takubar, *133, 134n.*
Takubar, 138, 142, 143, 144
Tamaluban, *87*
tambu, *see diwara*
Tanget, 103
Tani, native girl, *61n.*
taro: cultivation, *47, 105, 124*; trade, *25, 94*
Tavalai, *115n.*
tennis, *29*
Tetzlaff, trader, *48n.*
Thomas Cook Travel Agency, *135*
Thomas, Gordon, *147n., 148n.*
Tilmont family, *41, 42-3, 52, 60*
tobacco trade, *68, 69, 81-2, 93*
Togua, *115*
Tolai: *6, 20, 26*; material culture, *70-1*; social structure, *100-11*
totemism, *101-4*
trading, *46-7, 68-70, 81-2, 94, 98*
trepang, *see bêche-de-mer*
Triton Bay, *7*
tubuan, 106
turtle shell, *46, 47*

Uila, 'King', *118n., 136*
ukaukap, 107, 108

Vakubak, 110
Vancant, manager, *142*
Vatan, Father, *75*
Velaine, *33*
Vesters, Bishop, *147n.*
Vitu Islands, *122-3*
Vlavolo, *58n., 78, 91*
Vunakambambi, *58n., 85*
Vunanami, *70n.*

Waffler, trader, *132, 133*
wages, *26, 119-20*
Wahlen, Rudolph, *26, 128*
Wallis Island, *see* Lambom Island
Wallis, Samuel, *64n.*
watermelon, *52*
Watom Island, *121n.*
Western Australia, *9*
West Irian, *7, 46*
women, position of, *100-1, 105, 107*
Woodlark Island Mission, *74*
World War I, *130, 139-41*

Yap, *21*
Yekanavo, *28*
Ysabel, 85, 96, 117n.

Peter Biskup was born in Czechoslovakia and came to Australia in 1950 as a displaced person. He read law at the Comenius University, Bratislava, and is a graduate of the University of Western Australia. His first job in Australia was as a navvy; he also tried his luck as a gardener, furniture removalist, storeman, salesman and waiter.

Since 1958 he has worked in Perth as librarian and archivist, trained librarians at the National Library in Canberra, and taught history at the Administrative College of Papua and New Guinea. From 1969-72 he was Law Librarian at the Australian National University and now lectures in librarianship at the Canberra College of Advanced Education. He is co-author of *A Short History of New Guinea* (1968) and *Readings in New Guinea History* (1973) and author of *Not Slaves Not Citizens* (1973).

Designed by Philippa Walker, AIDIA

Printed letterpress in 10 point Monotype Baskerville one point leaded and printed on 85 gsm Burnie English Finish at The Griffin Press, Netley, South Australia